The English Patchwork

by
Pedro Tozzi

Illustrated by
Giovanna Lima

TBR Books
New York • Paris
Copyright ©2023 Pedro Tozzi
ISBN 978-1-63607-329-3
Library of Congress 2023935665

PREFACE

Why should we learn English through a natural method? This is the question teachers and students will be asking themselves when facing such a different and unique textbook of English as a Foreign Language. And the reason of course is the same as to why should we learn any language through a natural method? Yet given the number of different methods and textbooks of language learning available, any short answer simply would not be convincing. I believe a longer and hopefully better answer would go as follows.

The natural method was developed as a response to the now called grammar-translation method, which was used eminently for the teaching of Latin up until the mid-twentieth century, and frequently also today, because even though it hampers the development of speaking independence, it enables students to translate soon enough. In opposition to those, many methods were developed that prioritize speaking and avoid grammar explanations along with any interaction in the source language. But those traits were felt to have their consequences too, such as that students often struggled to grasp the meanings of news words and the logic behind most grammar rules. Besides, they did not fit most schools' curricula. And, of course, many other methods came later: the audio-lingual, which didn't thrive as much, and then the communicative, which was criticized for possibly leaving formal aspects of the target language unclear while prioritizing everyday interactions.

So, which is the best? It depends. Each has pros and cons and can be well or badly used for this or that objective, depending on the tools, textbook, student, and teacher. But the good news is that tempering is always possible and the weaknesses of each can be adapted and even solved. One can always balance advantages and use a more moderate and adequate approach for their ends. And that is why I started with "why should we learn English through a – not the – natural method?".

For, while The English Patchwork may look like a regular natural method textbook, it has been tempered by Mr. Tozzi's experience as a teacher not to slip into some of the method's weaknesses at all. It starts with the picture of a man, a woman, two boys and two girls, these words written below and their proper names written on top, before beginning with "Mrs. Johnson is a woman. Mr. Anderson is a man." – the most basic structure, along with a picture that makes it impossible to be misunderstood. Then, it gradually develops into the most common and important structures of English language, being understood and operated by the student right from the beginning, all of this with the aid of abundant pictures and explanation notes.

Besides a good beginning, it also solves a common problem of natural method textbooks, which is the lack of sufficient information in the side glossary for a good grasp of the text's meaning and grammatical structure. The English Patchwork is filled with all the information a student will need to comprehend its text, leaving no space for struggle. In the same way, all grammar rules introduced in a chapter are adequately explained in a dedicated section at its end, through vocabulary the student has already learned, and with the help of the side glossary, always widely clear about new structures as soon as they appear in text.

On top of that, the exercises will guarantee that the student has understood how to operate the new structures while practicing vocabulary (both new and known) and will provide the teacher with creative conversation starters for the classroom. Indeed, the exercises that close each chapter can easily be adapted to the context of the classroom, changing the names of the characters for the names of students, or situations of the story for situations of their lives, and so on, providing the perfect moment to exercise speaking and conversation while consolidating new content. One trait, among others, that works in this direction is the introduction of at least one new interrogative word each new chapter, enabling the teacher to dialogue with the students.

That much said, although it's safe to say that this text's method can most accurately be called natural, this is not what makes it an excellent tool for those who want to learn to speak English, but rather its being a textbook tempered with immersive situations, cohesive explanations, and fruitful exercises. In short, it succeeds in teaching a student how to operate the English language, in the same way that a person learns to operate a code: internalizing a set of symbols and learning how to combine them, and practicing doing so, so that learning new symbols or applying the code to new situations will never be a problem, at which point independency has been reached.

Of course, I could not forget to mention that all of that happens in the course of a fun story about a family whose children, after going through fun episodes in and out of their classroom, meet with other schoolmates in the cafeteria for a fascinating storytelling session. As a teacher of English, I believe this textbook has the potential to make lots of people enjoy learning in the immersive, effective, and nevertheless light and fun atmosphere The English Patchwork creates.

Enjoy!
Pietro Marchiori – ESL Teacher

TABLE OF CONTENTS

MRS. JOHNSON

JESSICA

JAMAL

SOPHIA

MICHAEL

MR. ANDERSON

WOMAN

GIRL

BOY

GIRL

BOY

MAN

Chapter 1

The Family

MRS. JOHNSON — WOMAN
JESSICA — GIRL
JAMAL — BOY
SOPHIA — GIRL
MICHAEL — BOY
MR. ANDERSON — MAN

Mrs. Mr.
Mrs. Johnson is a woman (♀)
Mr. Anderson is a man (♂)

is are
Jamal **is** a boy
Jamal and Michael **are** boys (**-s**)
Sophia and Jessica **are** girls (**-s**)

nor = and not

also
Sophia is a girl. Jessica is a girl.
= Sophia is a girl and Jessica
is **also** a girl.

no not
Is Jamal a girl?
No, he is a boy.

...?
Sophia is a girl. **(...is)/(...are)**
Is Sophia a girl? **(is...?)/**
(are...?)

yes ↔ no

he (♂) she (♀) they (♂/♀)
he **is** a boy / a man
she **is** a girl / a woman
they **are** boys / girls

Mrs. Johnson is a woman. Mr. Anderson is a man. Jamal is a boy. Michael is a boy. Sophia is a girl. Jessica is a girl. Jamal and Michael are boys. Sophia and Jessica are girls. Mrs. Johnson, Mr. Anderson, Jamal, Michael, Sophia, and Jessica are a family.

Mr. Anderson is not a woman. Mrs. Johnson is not a man. Jamal is not a girl. Sophia is not a boy. Jamal is not a girl, and Michael is not a girl. Jamal and Michael are boys. Sophia is not a boy. Sophia is a girl. Jessica is not a boy. Jessica is a girl. Sophia is not a boy, nor Jessica is a boy. Jamal is not a girl, nor Michael is a girl.

Jamal is a boy. Michael is a boy. Jamal is a boy, and Michael is also a boy. Sophia is a girl. Jessica is also a girl. Sophia is a girl, and Jessica is also a girl. Sophia and Jessica are girls. Jamal and Michael are boys.

Is Sophia a girl? Yes, Sophia is a girl. Is Jamal a boy? Yes, Jamal is a boy. Are Sophia and Jessica girls? Yes, Sophia and Jessica are girls. Are Jamal and Michael boys? Yes, Jamal and Michael are boys.

Is Mr. Anderson a boy? No, he is a man. Is Mrs. Johnson a girl? No, she is a woman. Are Jamal and Michael girls? No, Jamal and Michael are boys. They are boys. Are Sophia and Jessica girls? Yes, they are girls. Is Mr. Anderson a woman? No, he is a man. Is Jamal a boy? Yes, he is a boy. Is Sophia a girl? Yes, she is a girl.

Grammar
Singular (sing.) and plural (plur.)

Sophia **is** a girl. Sophia and Jessica **are** girls.
Jamal **is** a boy. Jamal and Michael **are** boys.
> **'is'**, **'boy'**, and **'girl'** are **singular** words.
> **'are'**, **'boys'**, and **'girls'** are **plural** words.

Gender: masculine (♂) and feminine (♀)

Mrs. Johnson is a **woman**. Sophia is a **girl**.
Mr. Anderson is a **man**. Jamal is a **boy**.
> **'woman'**, **'girl'**, and **'girls'** are **feminine (♀)** words.
> **'man'**, **'boy'**, and **'boys'** are **masculine (♂)** words.

Pronouns: he, she, and they

Jamal **is** a **boy**. **He** is a boy.
Mrs. Johnson **is** a **woman**. **She** is a woman.
Jamal and Michael **are boys**. **They** are boys.
Jessica and Sophia **are girls**. **They** are girls.
> **'He'** is a **masculine singular pronoun.**
> **'She'** is a **feminine singular pronoun.**
> **'They'** is a **masculine** and **also** a **feminine plural pronoun.**

Exercises

Mrs. Johnson is a __. Mr. Anderson is a __. Jamal is a __. Sophia is a __. Jamal __ Michael are boys. Sophia and Jessica __ girls. Mrs. Johnson, Mr. Anderson, Jamal, Michael, Sophia, and Jessica are a __

__ Sophia a girl? Yes, Sophia __ a girl. __ Sophia and Jessica girls? __, Sophia and Jessica are __.

Is Michael a girl? __, Michael is not a girl. __ Jamal a girl? No, Jamal is a __. Michael is not a girl, __ [:and not] Jamal is a girl.

Is Jessica a boy? No, __ [:Jessica] is not a boy. Is Jamal a boy? Yes, __ [:Jamal] is a boy. Are Sophia and Jessica girls? Yes, __ [: Sophia and Jessica] are girls. Sophia is a girl, and Jessica is __ a girl.

'He', 'she', and 'they' are __. 'He' is a __ singular pronoun. 'She' is a __ singular pronoun. 'They' is a __ and also a __ plural pronoun. 'He', 'boy', 'boys', and 'man' are __ words. 'She', 'girl', 'girls', and 'woman' are __ words.

'Boy' is a __ word. 'Boys' is a __ word. 'Girls' is also a __ word. 'Boy', 'girl', and 'man' are __ words. Is 'girl' a __ word? No, 'girl' is a feminine __. __ 'man' and 'woman' plural words? __, __ __ __ words. Is 'she' a masculine __? No, 'she' is a __ __

2.
Is Jamal a boy?
Is Jessica also a boy?
Is Mr. Anderson a man?
Is Mrs. Johnson a woman?
Are Sophia and Jessica girls?
Are Michael and Jessica boys?
Is 'he' a feminine pronoun?
Is 'girl' a masculine word?
Are 'boy' and 'girl' singular words?
Are 'boys' and 'girls' singular words?

---

boy woman
is girl
Jamal

'boy', 'woman', 'girl', 'is', and 'Jamal' are words.

singular = 1
plural = 2+

Gender
> Feminine gender: ♀
> Masculine gender: ♂

Words
also
and
Anderson
are
boy
chapter
exercise
family
feminine
girl
grammar
he
is
Jamal
Jessica
Johnson
man
masculine
Michael
Mr.
Mrs.
no
nor
not
plural
pronoun
she
singular
Sophia
they
woman
words
yes

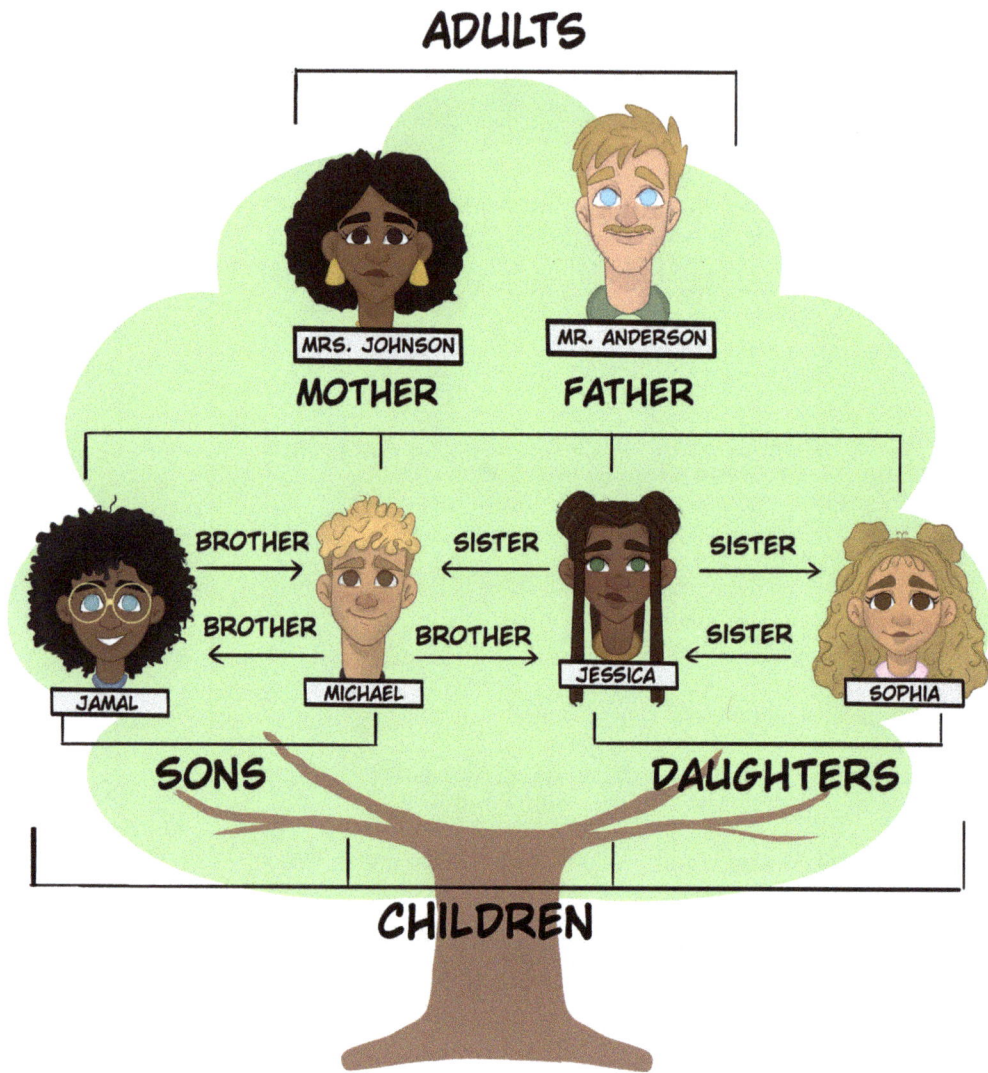

Chapter 2

The Family Tree

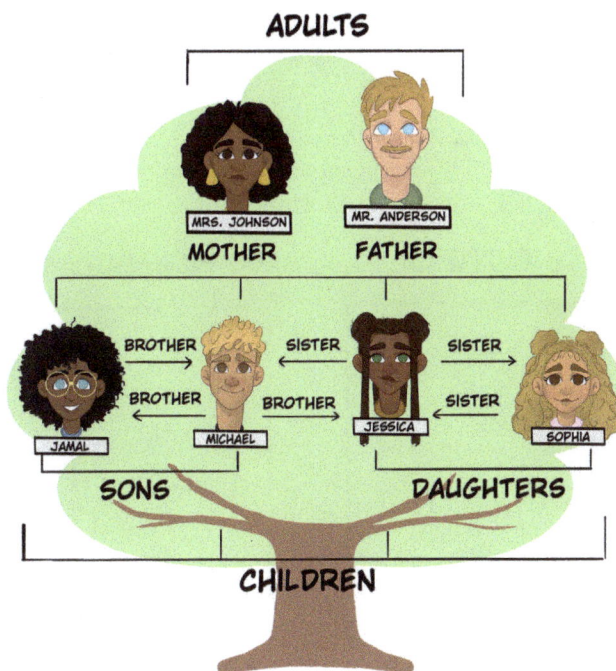

ADULTS

MRS. JOHNSON — MOTHER
MR. ANDERSON — FATHER

BROTHER → SISTER ← SISTER →
BROTHER ← BROTHER → SISTER ←

JAMAL — MICHAEL — JESSICA — SOPHIA

SONS — DAUGHTERS

CHILDREN

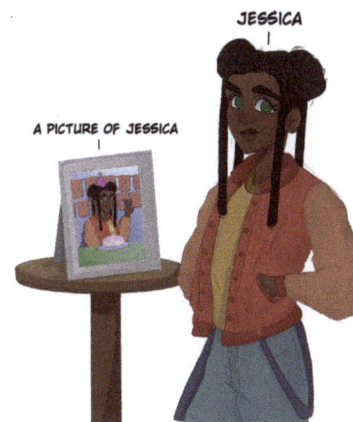

JESSICA

A PICTURE OF JESSICA

Mr. Anderson is a father. Mrs. Johnson is a mother. Jamal is a child, and Mr. Anderson is an adult. Sophia is also a child, and Mrs. Johnson is also an adult. The children are Jamal, Michael, Jessica, and Sophia. The adults are Mr. Anderson and Mrs. Johnson. The adults and the children are relatives. The family tree is a picture of the relatives of the family.

Jamal is the son of Mr. Anderson and of Mrs. Johnson. Jessica is the daughter of the adults. Sophia and Jessica are the daughters of the adults. The boys and girls are the sons and daughters of the adults, and the adults are the parents of the boys and girls. Sophia is the sister of Jessica, Jamal, and Michael. Jamal is the brother of Jessica, Sophia, and Michael.

Is Sophia a parent? No, Sophia is not. Sophia is the daughter of Mrs. Johnson. Jessica is the daughter of Mrs. Johnson too. Jamal is the son of Mrs. Johnson. Michael too is the son of Mrs. Johnson. Michael is also the brother of Jessica. Is Jessica the brother of Michael? No, Jessica is the sister of Michael. Jessica is a girl.

Whose son is Michael? Michael is the son of Mr. Anderson and of Mrs. Johnson too. Who is the father of Jamal? Mr. Anderson is the father of Jamal. Whose father is Mr. Anderson? He is the father of Jessica, Sophia, Jamal, and Michael. Whose parents are Mr. Anderson and Mrs. Johnson? They are the parents of the children. Is Sophia a relative? Yes, she is a relative of the family. Whose sister is Jessica? She is the sister of Sophia, Jamal, and Michael. Whose daughter is Jessica? She is the daughter of the adults.

Whose brother is Jamal? He is the brother of Jessica, Sophia, and Michael. Whose son is Jamal? He's the son of Mr. Anderson and of Mrs. Johnson too. Is Jessica the daughter of Mr. Anderson? Yes, she's the daughter of Mr. Anderson. Sophia is the daughter of Mr. Anderson too. They're the daughters of Mr. Anderson. Are Jamal and Michael the daughters of Mr. Anderson? No, they're the sons of Mr. Anderson. They are boys. Who are the sons of Mr. Anderson? Michael and Jamal are the sons of Mr. Anderson.

an = a
　an + a, e, i, o, h.
　a + **eu**, **u**-, b, c, d, f, g, h, j, k…

child, children
　She **is a child** (sing.)
　They **are children** (plur.)

relative = father, mother, sons, daughters...

a the
　Jamal is a son.
　Jamal is **the** son of Mr. A.

parent = father / mother
　Mr. Anderson is a parent
　Mrs. Johnson is a parent.
too = also

who...? whose...?
　who is the son of Mr. A.?
　　Michael is the son of Mr A.
　Whose son is Michael?
　　He is the son **of Mr. A.**

's 're

　He's = he is
　She's = she is
　They're = they are

Chapter 2 The Family Tree

Grammar
Articles

'a', 'an', and 'the' are **articles**
Michael is **a** boy
Mr. Anderson is **the** father of Michael

'a' is an **indefinite article**
'the' is a **definite article**

DEFINITE PICTURE

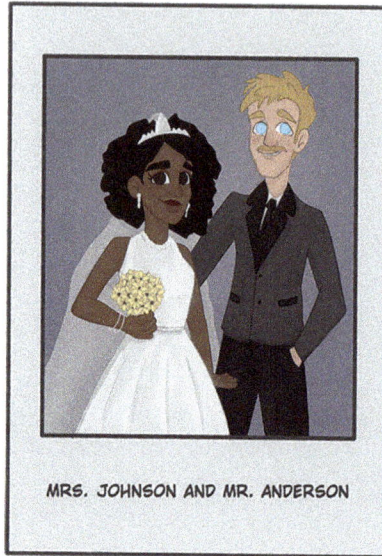

MRS. JOHNSON AND MR. ANDERSON

INDEFINITE PICTURE

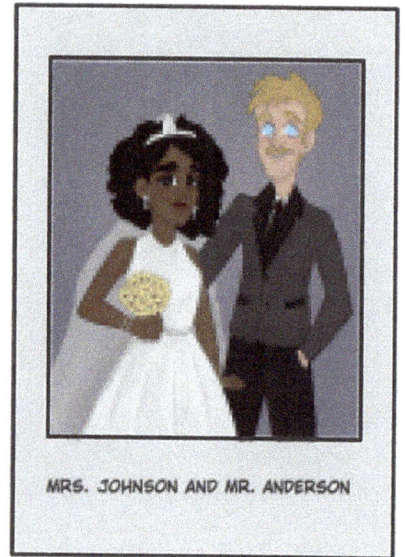

MRS. JOHNSON AND MR. ANDERSON

Relative Pronouns

Who is Michael? Michael is the son of Mr. Anderson.
Whose son is Michael? He is the son of Mr. Anderson.
Who are Jamal and Michael? They are the sons of Mrs. Johnson.
Whose son is Jamal? He is the son of Mr. Anderson and Mrs. Johnson

Whose...? ...of (singular and plural)
Who...? Mr. Anderson... (singular and plural)

Exercises

Michael is the __ of Mrs. Johnson. Jamal __ is the son of Mrs. Johnson. Jessica is the __ of Mrs. Johnson. Sophia is the daughter __ Mrs. Johnson too. Mrs. Johnson is the __ of Sophia. The boys and the girls are the__. Mr. and Mrs. Johnson are the __. The adults of the family are also the __ of the sons and daughters.

Michael is __ boy. Sophia is __ girl. Michael and Jamal are __ sons of Mr. Anderson. 'the' is __ article. 'a' is an article too. 'a', and 'an' are __ articles. 'The' is a __ article and 'a' and 'an' are __ articles.

The sons, the daughters, and the parents are __. The family __ is a __ of the relatives of the family. __ son is Jamal? He is __ son of Mrs. Johnson. __ is the mother of Sophia? __ __ is the mother of Sophia. Whose tree is the family tree? The family __ is a picture of the __ of the __.
Jamal is not __ adult. He is a __. Sophia is a child __. Whose __ is Sophia?

relative
  relative (family)
  relative (pronoun)

Words
a
an
adult
article
boys
brother
child
children
daughter
definite
indefinite
father
mother

She is the __ of Jessica. Who is Jamal? He is the __ of Michael and the __ of Mr. Anderson. __ brother is Michael? He is the brother __ Jamal, Sophia, and Jessica.

2.
Who is Jessica?
Whose daughter is Sophia?
Whose son is Jamal?
Is Mr. Anderson the father of Michael?
Whose mother is Mrs. Johnson?
Are Jessica and Sophia the sons of Mrs. Johnson?
Are Mr. Anderson and Mrs. Johnson children?
Are Jamal and Michael children?
Who is Sophia?
Is 'a' a definite article?
Is 'the' a definite article?

of
parent
picture
relative
sister
son
too
tree
who...?
whose...?

Chapter 3

In The House

— X IS IN THE HOUSE

X IS OUT OF THE HOUSE

Mr. Anderson and Mrs. Johnson are in the house. The boys, the girls, Max, and a tree are in the yard. Mr. Anderson and Mrs. Johnson are in the house. The girls, the boys, Max, and a tree are out of the house. Jamal is out of the house. Mr. Anderson is in the house.

Jamal is a person. Mr. Anderson is also a person. The boys, the girls, Mr. Anderson, and Mrs. Johnson are people. Mr. Anderson is a man. Mrs. Johnson is a woman. Jamal and Michael are not men, but boys. Sophia and Jessica are not women, but girls.

person (sing.) people (plur.)
    man (sing.) men (plur.)
    woman (sing.) women (plur.)
but
    Jamal is not a girl. Jamal is a boy.
    = Jamal is not a girl, **but**
    [Jamal is] a boy.

TALL TREE

SHORT TREE

Mr. Anderson is a tall man. Is Jamal tall? No, Jamal is not tall. He is short. Jamal is a short boy. Are Jamal and Michael men? No, they are not men. They are boys. Is Sophia tall? No, she is not tall. Sophia is a short girl. Is Jessica a short girl? No, she is tall girl. They are not women, but girls. Is Michael a tall boy? Yes, he is a tall boy. Michael is a tall boy, but Jamal is a short boy.

Is Max a person? No, it is not a person, nor the tree is a person. It is a tree. Max and the tree are not people. They are not people. Is Max in the house? No, it is not in the house. Is the tree in the house? No, it is in the yard. Are the boys and the girls in the yard? Yes, they are. Is Mr. Anderson in the yard? No, he is out of it. He's in the house.

it (Φ)
    Max is a dog. *It* is a dog.
Φ = not ♂ nor ♀.
Yes, they are [*in the yard*]
    it = the yard

Chapter 3 In The House

where...? ...in

it's = it is

How...like?
    big, small, short, tall...

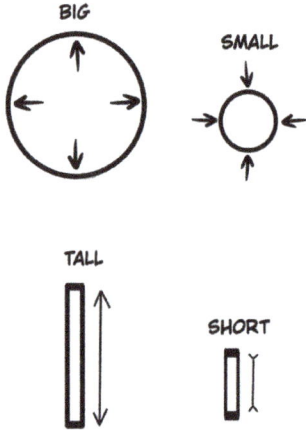

BIG

SMALL

TALL

SHORT

Jamal **says**: 'I am Jamal'

personal (adj.) < person

neuter gender (Φ) = not feminine nor masculine

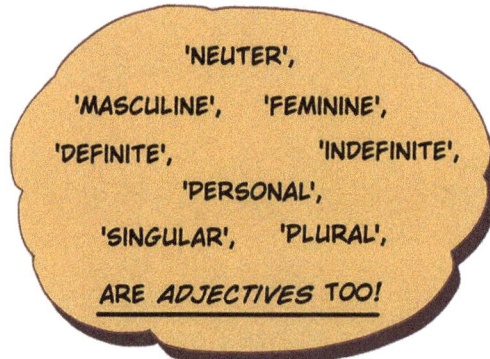

Where are the boys? They are in the yard. Where are the girls? They are in the yard too. Are Max and the tree in the house? No, they too are in the yard. Where are Mr. Anderson and Mrs. Johnson? They are not in the yard, but in the house. Is Max in the house? No, it's in the yard. Is the yard in the house? No, the yard is out of the house.

How is the yard like? The yard is big. The house is also big, but Max is small. Max is a small dog. Is Mr. Anderson big? No, Mr. Anderson is not a big man. He's a tall man. is Mrs. Johnson big? No, Mrs. Johnson is a small woman. How is Max like? Max is a small dog. How is the house like? The house is big.

Grammar
prepositions
    Sophia is **in** the house. The tree is **in** the yard.
    Jamal is **out** of the house. The dog is **out of** the yard.
        'in', and **'out [of]'** are **prepositions.**
        They say **'where'** a word is.

I AM JAMAL!

adjectives (adj.)
    Jamal is a boy. He is a **short** boy.
    Jessica is a girl. She is a **tall** girl.
    The house is **big**. It is a **big** house.
        'short', **'big'**, and **'tall'** are **adjectives.**
        They say **'how'** a word is **'like'**.

'NEUTER',
'MASCULINE',   'FEMININE',
'DEFINITE',   'INDEFINITE',
'PERSONAL',
'SINGULAR',   'PLURAL',
ARE ADJECTIVES TOO!

Personal pronouns (pers. pron.)
    The tree is out of the house. **It** is out of the house.
    Max and the tree are in the yard. **They** are in the yard.
    Jessica and Jamal are people. **They** are people.
        'It' is a **neuter singular personal pronoun.**
        'They' is a **plural personal pronoun.** (♂, ♀, and Φ)
        He', **'she'**, and **'it'** are **personal** pronouns too

A TALL BOY

A BOY

A SHORT BOY

Exercises

Mr. Anderson and Mrs. Johnson are __. Max is not a __. __ is a dog. Mr. Anderson is a __. Jamal and Michael are not __. __are boys. Mrs. Johnson is a __. Sophia and Jessica are not __. __ are girls. Max and the tree are not __. __ are not people.

__ are Max and the tree? They are __ the yard. The boys and the girls are __ the yard __. Where are the adults? __ are in the __. They are __ __ the yard.

Max is a __. __ is a dog. 'it' is a __ __ __ pronoun. 'neuter' is an __. 'tall', 'short', 'singular', and 'plural' are __ too. Max is in the __. 'in' is a __. 'out [of]' is also a __.

Max is not a person, __ a __. Mr. Anderson is a man, __ Mrs. Johnson is a woman. The boys are not __, nor the girls are __. Jamal is a boy, __ Jessica is a __.

How is the yard like? It is __. How is the house __? __ is __ too. How is Max like? __ is not __, but __. Is Mr. Anderson __? No, he is __, not big. Is Mrs. Johnson big? __, she's a __ woman.

Where are the boys and the girls? __ are __ the yard. They are not in the __. They are out of __ [: house].

2.

Is Max a person?
Where is Max?
Where are Mr. Anderson and Mrs. Johnson?
Are Jamal and Michael men?
Are Sophia and Jessica women?
Where are the children?
Where is the tree?
Is the dog in the house?
Is Michael a short boy?
Is Jessica a tall girl?
Is the word 'tall' and adjective?
How is the yard like?
How is the house like?
How is the tree like?

Words

adjective
big
but
dog
house
in
it
Max
men
neuter
out
people
person
personal
preposition
short
small
tall
where...?
women
yard
how...?

JAMAL AND SOPHIA
WALK TO THE SCHOOL.

Chapter 4

Occupations

JAMAL AND SOPHIA WALK TO THE SCHOOL.

Jamal walks to the school. Sophia walks to the school too. They walk to the school. Where are Jessica and Michael? They are in the house. Jessica and Michael do not walk to the school. Jessica does not walk to the school, nor does Michael.

Does Sophia walk to school? Yes, Sophia walks to school. Does Jamal walk to school? Yes, Jamal walks to school. Do Jamal and Sophia walk to school? Yes, they do. Does Michael walk to school? No, he does not. Michael doesn't walk to school. Do Michael and Jessica walk to school? No, they do not. They don't walk to school.

Do Mr. Anderson and Mrs. Johnson go to school? No, they don't. Mr. Anderson goes to the train station, and Mrs. Johnson goes to the fire station.

What is Mr. Anderson? He is a train driver. What does a train driver do? He drives the train. The train goes to the fire station. Mr. Anderson drives the train to the fire station. The fire station is far, but the school is close. The children walk to school, but Mr. Anderson drives to the fire station. The school is close to the House of Mr. Anderson, but the fire station is far from it.

Where is Mrs. Johnson? She is at the fire station. What is Mrs. Johnson? She is a firefighter. What does a firefighter do? She extinguises fires. Who is a firefighter? Mrs. Johnson is a firefighter. Firefighters extinguish fires. Mrs. Johnson is a firefighter, and Mr. Anderson is a train driver. She extinguishes fires, and he drives the train. How are the fires like? They're hot. The cold water extinguishes the hot fires.

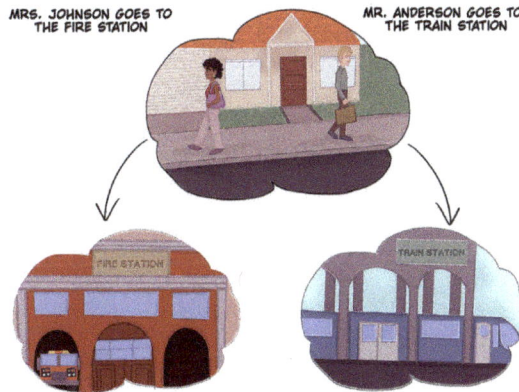

MRS. JOHNSON GOES TO THE FIRE STATION

MR. ANDERSON GOES TO THE TRAIN STATION

MRS. JOHNSON EXTINGUISHES THE FIRE

MR. ANDERSON DRIVES A TRAIN

Train driver' and 'firefighter' are occupations. What is the occupation of Jamal and Sophia? They are students. Children in schools are students. What do students do? They study. Sophia studies, and Jamal studies too. Whose occupation is 'firefighter'? The occupation of Mrs. Johnson is 'firefighter'. She extinguishes fires. Whose occupation is ' train driver'? The occupation of Mr. Anderson is 'train driver'. He drives trains. Whose occupation is 'student'? The occupation of Jamal, Sophia, Jessica, Michael… is 'student'. They're students. You are a student too. You study English!

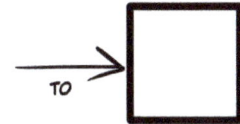

TO

walks walk
He / she / it **walks**
They **walk**

does do (not)
He / she / it **does** not walk
They **do** not walk

does do (…?)
does Sophia walk to school?
do the boys walk to school?
doesn't = does not
don't = do not
go = walk to
go, goes

what? who?
What is he? He is a driver.
Who is he? He is Mr. A.
Who…? …a person
What…? …**not** a person

at = in

A IS CLOSE TO B

A IS FAR FROM B

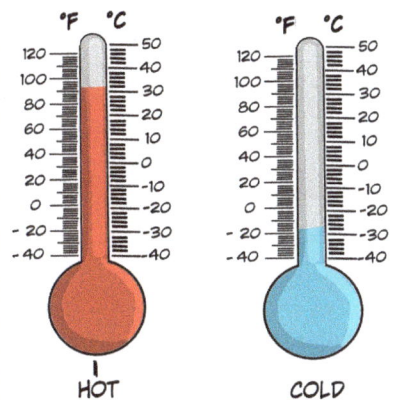

HOT   COLD

Chapter 4 Occupations

negative (adj.) < no
'no', 'not', 'nor' are
negative words

Interrogative (adj.) = ??
Where…? and Who…?
are **interrogative** words.

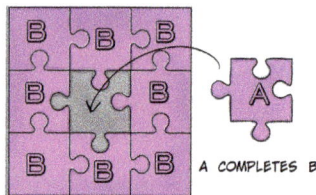

A COMPLETES B

Words

at	verb
close to	walk
cold	water
complete	what…?
do	
does	
don't	
doesn't	
driver	
drive	
extinguish	
far from	
fire	
firefighter	
go	
goes	
hot	
interrogative	
negative	
object	
occupation	
school	
station	
student	
study	
subject	
to	
train	

Grammar

Verbs

He **walks** to the school.
They **walk** to the school.
> 'walk' is a **verb. He/she/it** walks. **They** walk.
> Verbs say "**what**" a word **does**.

Verbs – Negative (+ **does** and **do**)
She **does not** walk to school.
They **do not** walk to school.

Verbs – Interrogative (**does**…? and **do**…?)
Do**es** it walk to school?
Do they walk to school?
> '**do**' and '**does**' are verbs. **He/she/it** does. **They** do.

Subject and object (subj. and obj.)
Mr. Anderson drives **the train.**
She extinguishes **the fire.**
> 'Mr. Anderson' and 'she' are **subjects.**
> The subject **does** the **verb.**
> 'the train' and 'the fire' are **objects.**
> The object **completes** the verb.

Exercises

Jamal and Sophia __ to the __. Jamal __ __ the school, but Michael __ not __ to the school. Michael __ [:does not] walk to the school. Jamal and Sophia __ to the school, but Jessica and Michael __ not __ to the school. Jessica and Michael __ [: do not] walk to the school.

Where is Mrs. Johnson? She is __ the __ __. Where is Mr. Anderson? He is at the __ __. What are they? She is a __ and he is a __ __. 'Firefighter' and 'train driver' are __. __ are Jamal and Sophia? They are __. Children in __ are students. What do students __? They __. Jamal __, and Sophia __ too. Jamal and Sophia walk __ the __. The school is __ to the house of Jamal and Sophia. Mr. Anderson drives the __ to the __ __. The fire station is __ from the __ __

What __ Mr. Anderson __? He __ the train to the fire station. The train __ (< go) to the fire station. __ is at the fire station? __ __ is at the fire station. She is a __. What do firefighters do? They __ __. How is fire like? __ is __. Water __ fires. How is the __ like? It is __.

Do the adults __ (< go) to school? No, they __ __ to the school. The __ (< child) go to the school. __ Mr. Anderson __ (< go) to school? No, he __ to the __ __. The fire station is __ __ the house of Mr. Anderson and of Mrs. Johnson. The children walk __ the __. The school is __ __ the __ of the children.

"Mrs. Johnson extinguishes the fire". 'Mrs. Johnson' is the __. 'extinguishes' is the __. 'the fire' is the __. The subject __ the verb. The object __ it. Are 'no' and 'not' __ words? Yes, __ are negative words. What are 'where…?', 'who…?' and 'what…?' They are __ words.

2.
How is fire like?
How is water like?
What does the water do?
What does Mrs. Johnson do?
What does Mr. Anderson do?
What do the children do?
What is the occupation of Mr. Anderson?
What is the occupation of Mrs. Johnson?
What are the children?
What does the object do?
What does the subject do?
Are 'where…?' and 'how…?' negative words?

Chapter 5

The Chat

A CHAT

who *else* is in the c.?
= who is in the c. too?
towards = to

I, my
Juan says: "I am Juan. Lucía is my sister" (Lucía is the sister of Juan)
I **am**, he/she/it **is**, they **are**

Where are Jamal and Sophia? They are in the classroom. The classroom is in the school. Who is in the classroom? Jamal and Sophia are in the classroom. Who else is in the classroom? Juan and Lucía are in the classroom too. Juan and Lucía are students too. Jamal walks towards Juan and Lucía.

Jamal says: "Hi, Lucía! This is my sister, Sophia." Lucía says: "Hi, Jamal! That is my brother, Juan." Juan walks towards the children, and says "Hi! I am Juan, and this is my sister, Lucía. She is my sister." Jamal says: "Hi, Juan! I am Jamal, and this is my sister, Sophia."

you, your
Sophia says: "Juan, you are the brother of Lucía. Lucía is your sister"

you **are**, your sister (= she) **is**

ask: ...? answer ...!

Sophia says: "Hi, Juan! Jamal is my brother. Is Lucía your sister?" Juan says: "yes, Lucía is my sister." And Juan asks: "are you the sister of Jamal, Sophia?" Sophia answers: "yes, I am the sister of Jamal. He is my brother."

Lucía asks: "who is your sister, Jamal?" Jamal answers: "Sophia is my sister. Jessica is my sister too, but Jessica is not here. Jessica is in my house. Sophia is here, but Jessica is not here." Lucía says: "My brother Juan is here, but my sister Carmela is not here. She is in my house. My mother is also there."

Whose sister is Carmela? She's Lucía's sister. Who is Juan? He's Lucía's brother. Juan is Lucía's brother and Lucía is Juan's sister. Is Jessica Jamal's sister? Yes, she's Jamal's sister. Is Jessica here in the classroom? No, Jessica is far from the classroom. She's in the house. Whose house is it? It's Jamal's, Sophia's, Jessica's, Michael's, Mr. Anderson's and Mrs. Johnson's house. It's the house of the family.

'*s* = of
    Lucia's = of Lucia
    Juan's = of Juan

"Where is the teacher?", asks Jamal? "There she is!", Juan answers. The teacher walks towards the students and says: "Hello, students!"

hello! = hi!

Grammar

Personal pronouns
    Jamal says: "**I** am Jamal". Lucía says: "**I** am Lucía".
    Jamal says: "**you** are a tall boy, Michael".
    Michael says: "**you** are a short boy, Jamal".
        '**I**' is a **first-person singular** personal pronoun.
        '**you**' is a **second-person singular** personal pronoun.
        '**he**', '**she**', and '**it**' are **third-person singular** pronouns.

Possessive adjectives (pos. adj.)
    Jamal says: "she is **my** sister Sophia" (Sophia is the sister of Jamal).
    Lucía says: "Sophia is **your** sister, Jamal. Juan is **my** brother".
        '**my**' is a **first-person possessive** adjective.
        '**your**' is a **second-person possessive** adjective.

Chapter 5 The Chat

Words

am
answer
ask
chat
classroom
close
demonstrative
else
far
first-person
hello!
here
hi!
I
Juan
Lucía
my
possessive
's
say
second-person
student
teacher
that
there
third-person
this
towards
you
your

Demonstrative pronouns

Jamal says: "**this** is my sister Sophia." Sophia is **close**.
Lucía says: "**that** is my brother Juan." Juan is **far**.
'**this**' and '**that**' are **demonstrative pronouns**.
'**this**' [house, tree, boy…] is **close**.
'**that**' [house, tree, boy…] is **far**.

Exercises

Jamal and Sophia are __ the __. Who __ is in the classroom? Juan and Lucía are there. Juan and Lucía are __. Jamal and Sophia walk __ Lucía. Jamal __: "__, Lucía! __ is my sister, Sophia". Lucía says: "__ (= hi!), Jamal! __ is __ brother Juan." Sophia is close __ __ and Juan is far __ __. Juan walks __ Lucía, Jamal, and Sophia. Juan __: who are you, Sophia? Sophia __: "__ __ the sister of Jamal. He is __ brother. Is Lucía __ sister?" Juan answers: yes, __ is __ __. I __ __ (< Lucía) brother.

Lucía says: "Jamal, __ are __ (< Sophia) __, and she is __ sister." Jamal says: "yes, Sophia is __ sister, and __ __ __ (< Sophia) brother." Lucía __: who __ is your sister, Jamal? He __: "Jessica is my sister too, but she __ not __. Jessica is in __ house. My sister Jessica is __ from the classroom, but __ sister Sophia is __ the classroom." Lucía says: "__ sister Carmela is also not __. She is in my house. My mother is __ too. My house is far __ the classroom. It is not __ to __.

'I', 'you', and 'he' are __ __. I __ a person. You __ a person. They are __. The __ singular personal pronoun is 'I'. The __ singular pronoun is 'you'. 'My', and 'your' are __ adjectives. 'This' and 'that' are __ __. Juan says: this is __. That is not close. That is __.

2.

Whose brother is Juan?
Whose sister is Lucía?
Is Jessica in the classroom?
Who is in the classroom?
Who else is in the classroom?
What does the teacher say?
What is the first-person singular personal pronoun?
What is the second-person singular personal pronoun?
What is the first-person singular possessive adjective?
What is the second-person singular possessive adjective?
What are the demonstrative pronouns?

THE TEACHER

Chapter 6

In Class

Chapter 6 In Class

THE TEACHER

in class = in the classroom

you all = you (plural)
we = you and I / you all and I
their (possessive adj.) < they

has have
> **I have**, you **have**, we **have**,
> you all **have**, they **have**
> he/she/it **has**

the answer < answer (verb)
you both = you 2
our your (possessive adj.)
> We have a blue book.
> **Our** book is blue
> You all have a blue book.
> **Your** book is blue.

his her its (possessive adj.)
> The color of the book is blue:
> **its** color is blue.
> The father of Sophia is Mr. A.:
> **her** father is Mr. A.
> The brother of Jamal is
> Michael: **his** brother is Mr. A.

The children are in class. Mrs. Honey, the teacher, says: "Hello, students! You all have books: Jamal has a blue book, Juan and Lucía have yellow books, and Sophia and I have green books. We have green books". Juan and Lucía have yellow books: their books are yellow.

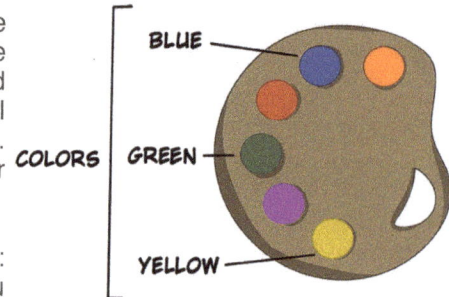

COLORS

BLUE

GREEN

YELLOW

The teacher asks: "Jamal, do you have a green book?" Jamal answers: "No, Mrs. Honey, I have a blue book". The teacher asks: "Sophia, do you have a green book?" Sophia answers: "Yes, Mrs. Honey, I have a green book. You have a green book too. We have green books". The teacher says "that is correct!".

The teacher asks: "Juan, what is the color of your book?" Juan answers: "it is a yellow book. I have a yellow book and Lucía has a yellow book too!". Teacher: "what is the color of your book, Lucía?" Lucía: "it is a green book". Teacher: "that is not correct. That is wrong." Lucía: "is my book yellow?" Teacher: "yes! that is the correct answer. You have a yellow book and Juan has a yellow book too. You both have yellow books."

Sophia asks: "what is the color of our books, Mrs. Honey?" Teacher: "our books are green, Sophia. Your book is green and my book is green too. What is the color of your books, Juan and Lucía?" Juan and Lucía answer: "our books are yellow!" Teacher: that is correct! What is the color of your book, Jamal?" Jamal: "my book is blue. I have a blue book."

Teacher: "Lucía, what is the color of Juan's book?" Lucía: "his book is yellow." Teacher: "what is the color of your sister's book, Juan?" Juan: "her book is yellow too!" Teacher: "this is my book. Its color is green. The color of this book is green. Juan and Lucía have yellow books. What is the color of their books?" Students: their books are yellow!

28

Reader, what is the color of your book? Your book, *The English Patchwork*, is multicolored. Patchwork is multicolored!

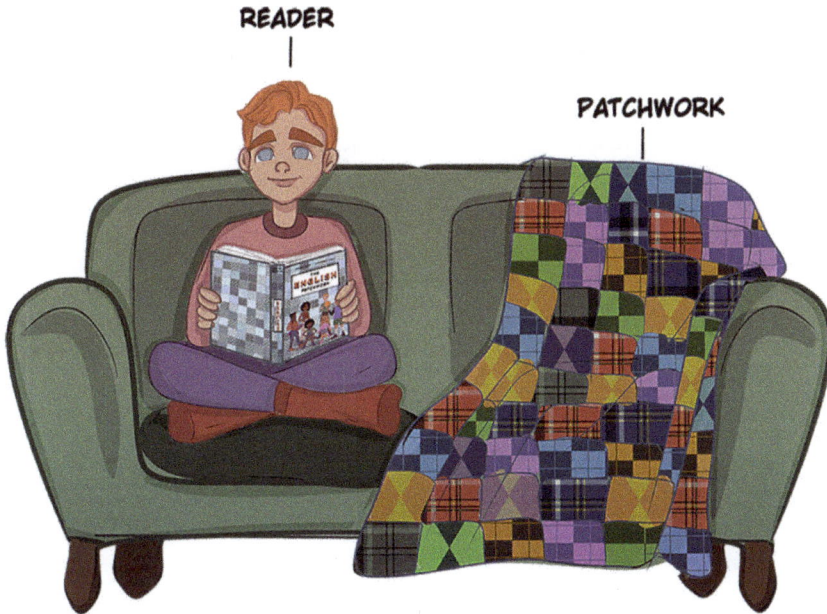

its ≠ it's
    its = possessive adjective < it
    it's = it is

READER

PATCHWORK

THE ENGLISH PATCHWORK IS A MULTICOLORED BOOK.

Grammar
Personal pronouns and their possessive adjectives

		PERSONAL PRONOUN	POSSESSIVE ADJECTIVE
SINGULAR	FIRST-PERSON	I	MY
	SECOND-PERSON	YOU	YOUR
	THIRD-PERSON	HE/SHE/IT	HIS/HER/ITS
PLURAL	FIRST-PERSON	WE	OUR
	SECOND-PERSON	YOU ALL	YOURS
	THIRD-PERSON	THEY	THEIR

possessive (adj.) < possess (verb).
    I, you, we, you all, they
    possess
    he/she/it **possesses**
    I possess = I have

We **possess** a book. It is our book.
They **possess** a book. It is their book.
He **possesses** a book. It is his book.

Chapter 6 In Class

Words

blue
book
both
class
color
correct
green
has
have
her
his
its
our
Mrs. Honey
patchwork
possess
reader
their
we
wrong
yellow
you all

Exercises

Jamal says: __ __ a blue book. Juan and Lucía __: __ __ yellow books. What is the __ of Juan's and Lucía's books? The color of __ books is __. What is the color of Jamal's book? __ color is __. Jamal __ a blue book. Sophia and the teacher say: __ __ green books. What is the color of their books? the color of their books is __. Teacher: what is the color of __ books, Juan and Lucía? Juan and Lucía: the color of __ books is __. Teacher: "that is __! __ __ (= 2) have yellow books. Children, you __ have books, but Juan and Lucía __ yellow books.

Teacher: Jamal, what is the color of __ book? Jamal: "it is yellow!" Teacher: "this __ is __ (= not correct). __ __ a blue book, Jamal, not a yellow book!" Jamal: "that is correct. I __ (= have) a blue book. Does Lucía possess a blue book?" Teacher: "Lucía __ (< do) not possess a blue book. She __ a __ book."

Teacher: "students, __ all __ books. I __ a book too. __ __ books. Does Sophia __ a book?" Students: "yes, she __ a book." Teacher: "what is the color of __ book?" Students: "__ color is __". Teacher: "does Jamal have a book?" Students: "yes, Jamal __ a book". Teacher: "what is the color of __ book?" Students: "its __ is blue.

2.

What is the color of Jamal's book?
What is the color of Sophia's book?
What is the color of Juan's and Lucía's books?
What do the children have?
Whose book is blue?
Whose books are yellow?
What is the color of the teacher's book?
What are the singular possessive adjectives?
What are the singular personal pronouns?
What are the plural possessive adjectives?
What are the plural personal pronouns?

BLACKBOARD

ONE THREE FIVE SEVEN NINE

1 3 5 7 9

0 2 4 6 8

ZERO TWO FOUR SIX EIGHT

Chapter 7
Numbers

Chapter 7 Numbers

THE TEACHER POINTS AT THE RED BOOK.

those = that (plur.)
that number I
those numbers

these = this (plur.)
this number I
these numbers

THE 🟠 IS ON THE 🟩.

great! = Yes! That
is correct!

How many...? zero (0), one (1),
two (2), three (3)...

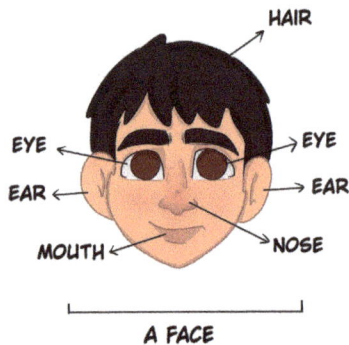

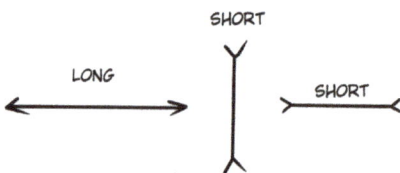

HAIR

EYE — — EYE
EAR — — EAR
MOUTH — — NOSE

A FACE

SHORT

LONG   SHORT

many   much
  In class are **many** student**s**.
  Jamal has **much** hair.
  many = 1, 2, 3...
  much = tall, long...
  (no number!)
both...and... = and...and...
The **teacher teach**es
there is, there are
  there is a student in class
  = one student is in class;
  there are two students in
  class = two students are in
  class

Mrs. Honey points at the blackboard and says: "this is the number one. That is the number two. Sophia, what numbers are in the blackboard?" Sophia: "zero, one, two, three, four, five, six, seven, eight, nine. Those are the numbers on the blackboard." Teacher: "that is correct. Jamal, what are these numbers close to the number one?" Jamal points at the numbers close to one and says: "those are the odd numbers, Mrs. Honey: one, three, five, seven, and nine". Teacher: "yes, those are the odd numbers. And what are those numbers close to the number zero, Lucía?" Lucía points at the numbers close to zero and says: "those are the even numbers: zero, two, four, six, and eight". Teacher: "great!"

Teacher: "I count the number of my eyes: One…, two… I have two eyes. How many eyes do you have, Juan?" Juan counts the number of his eyes: "one…, two…" and answers: "I have two eyes, teacher. How many ears do we have?" The teacher answers: "Alone, I have two ears. Together, you and I have four ears. How many mouths do you have alone, Jamal?" Jamal answers: "I have one mouth alone". Teacher: "and how many do you, Sophia, and I have together?" Jamal counts the number of mouths: "one, two, three", and says: "together, we have three mouths. Sophia has her mouth, I have my mouth, and you have your mouth. Those are three mouths together!" Teacher: "how many mouths and noses do we have together, Sophia?" Sophia: 'together, we have two mouths and two noses. I have my mouth and my nose, and you have your mouth and your nose too!"

A RED BOOK ALONE

A RED BOOK AND
A GREEN BOOK TOGETHER

Teacher: "this is my hair. That is your hair, Juan. How is it like?" Juan: "my hair is short, but your hair is long, teacher. My sister's hair is long too!" Teacher: "that is correct. Jamal, how much hair do you have?" Jamal: "I have much hair, but Juan has little hair." Teacher: "great! Juan's hair is short. He does not have much hair. Your hair is long, Jamal. You have much hair."

The students count the number of their eyes, mouths, noses, and ears, both alone and together. The teacher teaches the numbers and counts the numbers too, but she does not count her hair, nor do the students count their hair. We say: "I have much hair." We do not count hair. We say: "There are many students in class." We count the students: "one, two, three, four five…". We also say: there is one mouth in the face; we count it: "one…"

Grammar

Nouns and Verbs

The **stud**ent **stud**ies. The **teach**er **teach**es
Jamal **is** a student

'**student**', '**teacher**', and '**Jamal**' are **nouns**.
The noun is **a person, a dog, a tree...**
'**study**' and '**teach**' are **verbs**; '**is**' is a **verb** too.
'**am, is, are**' are **linking verbs**. They **link two nouns.**

Demonstrative pronouns

	SINGULAR	**PLURAL**
CLOSE (1st and 2nd person)	THIS	THESE
FAR (3rd person)	THAT	THOSE

Countable and uncountable nouns

Many students are in class. There are **five (5)** students in class.
Jamal has **much** hair. Juan has **little** hair.

'**Students**' is a **countable** noun.
We say: "there are **many** students here"
'**hair**' is an **uncountable** noun. We say: "I have **much** hair".
Uncountable nouns are **singular**. We do not say: ~~'hairs'~~

LINK
↓
NOUN━━━━━●NOUN

THE LINK LINKS THE NOUNS

the link (noun) I link (verb) I
linking (adj.)

demonstrative (adj.) <
demonstrate (verb)
   demonstrate = point at

countable ↔ *uncountable* < count
   '**students**' is a countable
   noun. We count the **number** of
   students: "one, two, three..."
   '**hair**' is an uncountable noun
   We do not count **the number**
   ~~of hairs~~.

Chapter 7 Numbers

Words

zero (0)
one (1)
two (2)
three (3)
four (4)
five (5)
six (6)
seven (7)
eight (8)
nine (9)
alone
blackboard
count
countable
counts
demonstrate
ears
even
eyes
great!
hair
how many...?
how much...?
uncountable
link (noun and verb)
linking
little
long
many
mouth
much
nose
noun
number
odd
point at
teach
these
those
together

Exercises

__ __ students are in class? There are __ students in class. How many eyes __ Sophia have? She has __ eyes. How many noses? Sophia has __ nose. Jamal has one nose too, but Jamal and Sophia have two __ __ (↔ alone). How many ears does Juan __? He has __ ears __ (↔ together). How many ears do Sophia and Juan have together? Together, they have __ __.

The teacher __ __ the numbers on the __. The __ 1, 3, 5, 7, and 9 are close to the teacher, but the numbers 0, 2, 4, 6, and 8 are far from the teacher. She says: "__ are the __ numbers. __ are the __ __." Jamal asks: __ are the even numbers? Teacher: "__, __, __, __, and __" Sophia __: "what are the odd numbers?" Teacher: __, __, __, __, and __. Sophia __ the __ numbers: "1, 3, 5, 7, 9".

Juan: "I have __ __. Jamal has __ hair." Sophia: "__ __ hair do you have, Lucía?" Lucía: "I have much __. My hair is __." Teacher: "Great!".

The teacher __ the numbers. "The English Patchwork" teaches the __ pronouns and the __ and __ nouns. 'Hair' is an __ noun. 'Students', '__', '__', '__'and 'ear' are __ nouns. Is 'countable' a __? No, it is an adjective. Is 'am, is, are' an adjective? No, it is a __ __. Linking verbs __ two __.

2.

What are the even numbers?
What are the odd numbers?
How many eyes do you have?
How many noses do you have?
How much hair do you have?
Do you have many mouths?
Do you count your hair?
What does the teacher do?
Where is your hair?
Where is your nose?
Where is your mouth?
Is 'am, is, are' a noun?
Is there one nose in the face?
Are there two mouths on the face?

Chapter 8

The Telephone Game

Chapter 8 The Telephone Game

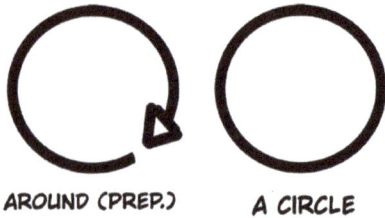

AROUND (PREP.)   A CIRCLE

-ly
    A loud volume (adjective + noun)
    I loudly say (ad**verb** + verb)
phrase = many words together
whisper [**to** a person] = quietly say [**to** a person]
I listen **to**
and so on
    1, 2, 3, 4... = 1, 2, 3, 4, and so on

BEGINNING

END

begin (verb) < the beginning (noun)
set sail = I begin **to** go (on a ship)
salty (adj.) < salt (noun)...

TELEPHONE GAME

A TELEPHONE

TABLE

The children sit around the table in a circle. Mrs. Honey, the teacher, loudly says: "this is the Telephone Game! I whisper a phrase to Jamal. For example: *here is a blue book*. Jamal listens to the phrase and whispers it to Lucía: *here is a blue book*. Lucía listens to Jamal and whispers to Juan: *here is a blue book*, and so on...

In the beginning, I whisper to you, Jamal, and you listen to me. Jamal whispers to Lucía, and Lucía listens to him. Lucía whispers to Juan, and Juan listens to her, and so on.
In the end, Sophia whispers to me, and I loudly say the phrase to you all.

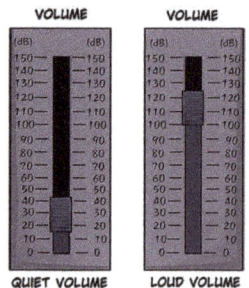

VOLUME   VOLUME

QUIET VOLUME   LOUD VOLUME

The game begins. The teacher whispers this phrase to Jamal:

The sailors on the ship set sail in the salty sea waves

WAVES

SAILORS

SHIP

SALT

SEA   SET SAIL

Jamal listens to her and whispers to Lucía:

The sailors on the sheep set sail on the salty sea waves

SHE IS CONFUSED

Jamal doesn't say the same phrase as the teacher. Jamal whispers another phrase to Lucía. He changes the phrase.

Lucía confusedly listens to Jamal, but correctly whispers the same phrase to Juan. She does not change the phrase:

The sailors on the sheep set sail on the salty sea waves

Juan doesn't understand her correctly. Juan whispers an incorrect phrase to Sophia. He whispers another phrase, not the phrase Lucía whispers. He changes the phrase:

The sailors on the sheep set sail and sadly see wafers

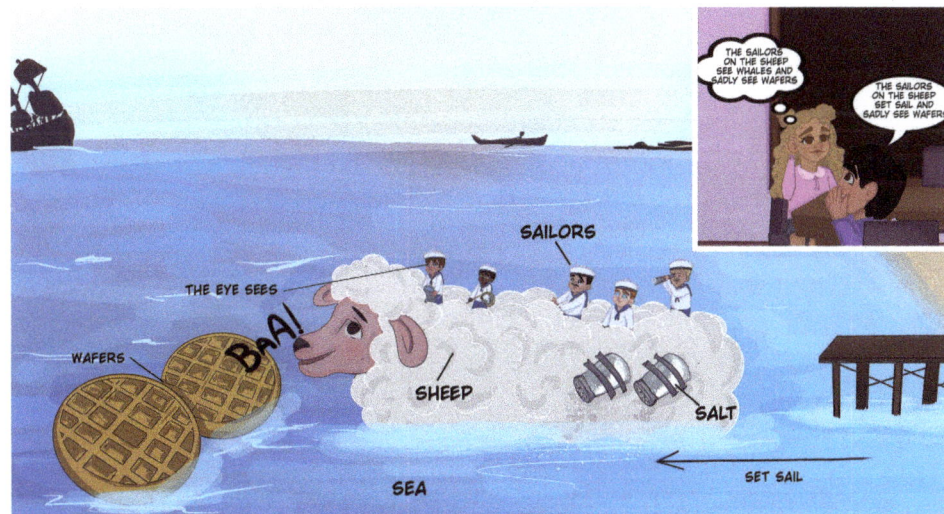

ship ≠ sheep

A BOOK   THE SAME BOOK   ANOTHER BOOK

The red book is the same **as** the red book, but not the same **as** the green book

correctly < correct
understand = listen correctly

HE IS SAD

hear (a person / word) = listen to
(a person / word)

joyful ↔ sad

SHE LAUGHS

modify = change

me < I
him, his < he, she
you / you all (obj. pron) < you /
you all (pers. pron.)
or ↔ and

AN EYE IS BROWN OR GREEN OR BLUE

THE BOOK IS BROWN AND GREEN AND BLUE

Words
adverb
another
around
as
begin (verb)
beginning (noun)
brown

Sophia incorrectly hears him too, and whispers another phrase to the teacher. She changes the phrase.

The sailors on the sheep see whales and sadly see wafers

The teacher laughs joyfully: ha ha ha! and loudly says Sophia's words to the students. Do you play the Telephone Game too? Do you change the phrases?

Grammar
Adverbs
Jamal is a **joyful** boy. Jamal joyful**ly** says: "Hi, Sophia!"
Jamal's answer is **correct.** He answers correct**ly**.
'**quietly**', and '**correctly**', are **adverbs (-ly)**. The adverb **modifies** the verb;
(The adverb modifies the adjective, a phrase, and another adverb too)

Object Pronouns (obj. pron.)
I say a phrase **to Jamal**, and another **to Sophia**.
= I say a phrase **to him**, and another **to her**.
Teacher: "Jamal *whispers* a phrase **to me**. I *whisper* a phrase **to you**, Lucía"
Jamal: "I *whisper* a phrase **to you [all]**, Juan and Sophia."
    '**me**', '**him**', '**her**', '**you [all]**' are **object pronouns.**
    They are the **object** of a *verb or preposition*

Exercises
The students sit __ the __ in a __ (= 'O'). The Telephone Game __ (↔ end):

Mrs. Honey __ (= quietly says) to Jamal: *the __ on the __ set sail in the __ (< salt) sea waves*. Jamal __ __ the teacher and correctly says the __ (↔ another) phrase to Lucía: *the sailors on the ship __ __ in the salty __ __*. Does Lucía understand __ (= Jamal)? No, she doesn't: she __ (↔ correct) whispers to Sophia: *the sailors on the __ (baa!) set sail on the salty sea waves*.

Sophia __ (= listen to) Lucía. Does Sophia understand __ (= Lucía)? Yes, she does, but she is __ (= ???). Sophia correctly whispers to Juan: *the sailors on the sheep set sail on the salty sea waves*. Juan is confused too! Does he say the same phrase __ Sophia? No, he doesn't: he says __ phrase: *the sailors on the sheep see __ and __ (↔ joyful) see wafers*.

Chapter 8 The Telephone Game

Teacher: Juan, whisper the phrase to __ (< I), and I whisper it to __ __ (< you (plur.)). Juan whispers the phrase to the Teacher, and she __ __ (↔ whisper) it to the students: *the sailors on the sheep see whales and sadly* __ (what does the eye do?) *wafers.* The students __ (↔ sad) __: ha ha ha! The Telephone __ __ (↔ begin).

Sophia, Jamal, Lucía, Juan, and the Teacher __ the Telephone Game. Sophia whispers to Jamal, Jamal to Lucía, Lucía to Juan, __ __ __...

What are __? *Joyfully* and *sadly*, for __, are adverbs. *Loudly* is an example of adverb too. What does the adverb 'loudly' do in the phrase: *Jamal loudly answers?* The adverb __ the verb *answers.*

What is the word *me* in the phrase *Jamal whispers a phrase to me?* It is an __ pronoun. The object pronouns are *me, him,* and *her,* __ example. The object pronoun is the object of a verb __ preposition.

2.
How is the sea like?
Who sets sail?
Where do we set sail?
What do we play?
What are many words together?
How do we whisper?
Is sheep the same as ship?
Is whale the same as wafer?
Do you hear the phrase correctly?
How do you laugh?
Around what do the students sit?
What color is your book?

change
circle
confused
end
for example
game
hear
him
incorrect
joyful
laugh
listen to
loud
-ly
me
modify
on
or
phrase
playa
quiet
red
sad
set sail
sailor
salt
salty
same
say
sea
see
sheep
ship
sit
and so on...
table
telephone
understand
volume
wafer
wave
whale
whisper

TIME	CLASS
9:00	MRS. SMITH'S
10:00	MRS. HONEY'S
11:00	RECESS
11:30	MR. MARTIN'S
12:00	MRS. WILLIAMS'

BEFORE CLASS
WITH MRS. HONEY

↑
↓

AFTER CLASS
WITH MRS. HONEY

Chapter 9

Recess

TIME	CLASS
9:00	MRS. SMITH'S
10:00	MRS. HONEY'S
11:00	RECESS
11:30	MR. MARTIN'S
12:00	MRS. WILLIAMS'

BEFORE CLASS WITH MRS. HONEY
AFTER CLASS WITH MRS. HONEY

After class with Mrs. Honey, it is recess time! When is class with Mrs. Honey? It is at ten o'clock. When is recess? Recess is at eleven (11) o'clock. Recess is after class with Mrs. Honey.

After recess, students go to Mr. Martin's class. When is Mr. Martin's class? It is at eleven-thirty (11:30). Mr. Martin's class is before Mrs. Williams' class. Mrs. Williams' class is at twelve (12) o'clock. Mrs. Williams teaches at twelve o'clock, and Mr. Martin teaches at eleven-thirty. Mr. Martin teaches before Mrs. Williams, and Mrs. Williams teaches after Mr. Martin.

At what time does Mrs. Smith teach? She teaches at nine o'clock. Does Mrs. Smith teach before Mrs. Honey? Yes, she teaches right before Mrs. Honey. Does Mrs. Smith teach right before recess? No, Mrs. Honey teaches right before recess. Recess is right after Mrs. Honey's class. Whose class is right before recess? Mrs. Honey's class is right before recess. Whose class is right after recess? Mr. Martin's class is right after recess.

During recess, Juan and Sophia see Bradley, Alessandra, Xiang and Hannah. They say "Hi! Do you all want to play with us?". Hannah and Xiang answer: "yes, we want to play with you all!" What game do you all want to play?". Juan and Sophia answer: "we want to play Guess What?".

Not all students, however, want to play with Juan and Sophia. Bradley and Alessandra say: "we don't want to play right now. We want to eat."

Alessandra and Bradley eat. While they eat, the other children play.

Sophia says: *What is long and heavy and sails on the sea?*

The students try to answer Sophia's question. Juan guesses: "is it a whale?" Sophia says: "a whale is long and heavy, but you guess incorrectly, Juan! A whale doesn't sail. A whale swims!" Hannah guesses: "is it a ship?" Sophia answers: "yes! A ship is long and heavy, and sails on the sea."

recess ↔ class
when...? at...
   when...? = at what time?
o'clock = :00 (time)
   seven o'clock = 7:00
   ten o'clock = 10:00
s' (< 's)
   Mrs. Williams'
   (= Mrs. Williams's)
after (adv.) ↔ before (adv.)

right (adv.)
   9:00 is right before 9:01
   9:01 is right after 9:00

during r. = at the same time when
   r. is
us (obj. pron.) < we

all
   There are 6 students →
   all students = 6 students
however = but
now = at this time

while (+ phrase) = during
(+ noun)
   during *recess* (noun)
   while *they play* (phrase: subj.
   and verb)
other (sing. / plur.) < another (sing.)
   another < a + other
   the other child / children

sail = go on a ship in the sea
I try, he/she/it tri**es**
can ↔ cannot
   cannot < can not
   I / you / we / you all / they can
   he / she / it **can** (not he
   ~~cans~~)
ask us a question = ask a
   question *to us*

them (obj. pron.) < they
it (obj. pron.) < it
always = at all times
be < am, is, are
　　It is a color. It can be green,
　　or red, or brown…

for (prep. + time) = during that
　　time
I call Juan = I say: "Juan!"
to be over ↔ to begin

to guess complements the verb. It
　　is an **object** of the verb 'try'.

to guess is an infinitive.
It is a verb too!
　　The correct answer is the
　　object of the infinitive
To be over does the verb.
　　It is a **subject.**
the complement < complete
be (inf.) < am, is, are

Juan tries to answer Sophia's question, but cannot answer correctly. Hannah tries to answer the same question, and she can answer correctly. Sophia says: "You guess correctly, Hannah! Now you ask us a question."

The students listen to Hannah. She asks a question to them. What is the correct answer? Can the students guess it?

What is always light and can be long or short?

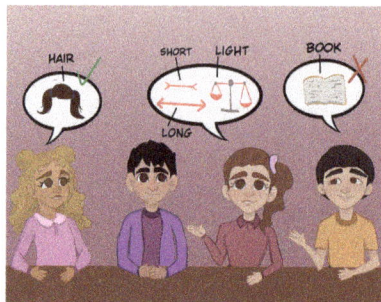

Xiang guesses: "is it a book?" Hannah says: "a book can be long or short, but a book can be heavy too! You guess it incorrectly, Xiang." Can Sophia guess it correctly? She guesses: "is it hair?". Hannah answers: "yes! Hair is always light, but can be long or short. Juan's hair is short, but my hair is long."

The students joyfully play for a long time. When recess is over, the teacher calls them: "Students! recess is over! It is eleven-thirty. Mr. Martin's class begins! Juan says: "the teacher calls us! Recess is sadly over…"

Grammar
Infinitive (inf.)

'to guess', 'guess', and 'be' are **infinitives**
Infinitives with 'to' can be the **object** or **subject** of a verb
(but not of a preposition!)
Infinitives with no 'to' can **complement** a verb.
They can be the **object** of the verb.
Infinitives are verbs too! They can have an object, but **no person**

Object Pronouns

		PERSONAL PRONOUN	OBJECT PRONOUN
SINGULAR	FIRST-PERSON	I	ME
	SECOND-PERSON	YOU	YOU
	THIRD-PERSON	HE/SHE/IT	HIM/HER/IT
PLURAL	FIRST-PERSON	WE	US
	SECOND-PERSON	YOU ALL	YOU ALL
	THIRD-PERSON	THEY	THEM

Exercises

Mr. Martin teaches at __ (11:30). Recess is at __ __ (11:00). Recess is __ before Mr. Martin's class, and his class is right __ recess. Mrs. Williams teaches at __ o'clock (12:00). Mr. Martin's class is right __ her class. When is Mrs. Williams_ class? It is at twelve __ (12:00). When is Mrs. Honey's class? It is right before __. Her class is at __ __ (10:00).

It is eleven o'clock. Recess __ (↔ ends)! Recess begins at eleven o'clock, and __ __ (= ends) at twelve o'clock. __ (= at the same time when…) recess, the kids joyfully play! Juan and Sophia __ Xiang, Hannah, Alessandra, and Bradley: "Xiang! Hannah! Alessandra! Bradley!". They ask: "do you all want __ __ with __ (< we)? Xiang and Hannah answer: yes! We __ to play with __ __ (< you all). Bradley and Alessandra, __, do not __ to play __ (= together) __ (< they). They say: 'we do not __ __ __ with __ __ (< you all). We want __ __ (yum yum!). Alessandra and Bradley eat together: Alessandra eats __ Bradley, and Bradley eats __ Alessandra. __ (at the same time when…) they eat, the __ children play.

Sophia asks: "what is __ (↔ light) and __ (↔ short), and __ (= begins to set sail) on the sea?". Juan __: "is it a whale"? Sophia says: "this in incorrect, Juan. A whale is heavy and long, but a whale doesn't sail. A whale __!" Hannah __ to guess __ (< it): "is it a ship?". Sophia joyfully answers: "yes! You answer __, Hannah!".

Hannah asks: "what is __ (= at all times) __ (↔ heavy) and can be long or __ (↔ long)?". Can the students guess __? Sophia guesses: "is it a book?". Hannah answers: "no, you guess it incorrectly, Sophia. A book __ __ long or short, but can be light or heavy too. A book is not always light." Xiang tries __ __ it too: "is it hair?" Hannah answers: "yes! Hair can be long or short, but is always light!"

Xiang asks: "what can be __ or green or blue?" Juan guesses: "is it an eye?" Xiang answers: "yes! You answer correctly!"

The children play __ a long __. When recess is over, the teacher calls __ (< they): "students! Recess is over! __ (= at this time) it is eleven-thirty. Mr. Martin's class begins!"

2.

When is Mr. Martin's class?
When is Mrs. Honey's class?
What can be brown or blue or green?
What does a whale do?
What do Bradley and Alessandra do during recess?
What do the other children do during recess?
What is always light, but can be short or long?
What are the words "to be", "to guess"…?

Words

after
Alessandra
all
always
be (inf.)
before
begin
Bradley
brown
call
can
cannot
complement
during
eat
eleven (11)
-thirty (xx:30)
for
guess
Hannah
heavy
however
infinitive
light
Mr. Martin
now
o'clock
other
over
recess
right (adv.)
s'
sail
Mrs. Smith
swim
them
time
try
twelve (12)
us
want
when...?
while
Mrs. Williams
with
Xiang

Chapter 10

Physical Education Class

Chapter 10 Physical Education Class

The students are at the gym with Mr. Martin. How is he like? He is a tall, big man. He always plays in the gym. He teaches Physical Education. In P.E. class, students play in the gym. Mr. Martin says: "Sophia and Juan, pick two teams!"

GOAL   GOAL

JUAN'S TEAM   SOPHIA'S TEAM

THE GYM

Mr. Martin commands Sophia and Juan to pick two teams. Sophia and Juan have to pick two teams. There are twelve students in class. Sophia and Juan call each student to a team. Sophia calls: "Xiang!". Juan calls: "Hannah!". Sophia calls: "Jamal!". Juan calls: "Alessandra!", and so on. Now, each team has six students. Sophia's team has six students and Juan's team has six students too.

command to pick = say: "pick!"
each = all
    There are 6 students:
    all = 6 students
    each = 1+1+1+1+1+1
    each is always singular
now = at this time

THROW

BALL

CATCH

Mr. Martin says: "great! Sophia, your team begins. Catch!". While he says 'catch!', Mr. Martin throws the ball to Sophia. Sophia has to catch the ball. Can she catch the ball? Yes, she can catch the ball. Mr. Martin says: "we play Handball. Each team has to throw the ball at the goal of the other team."

THROW AT

Handball < hand + ball

A HAND

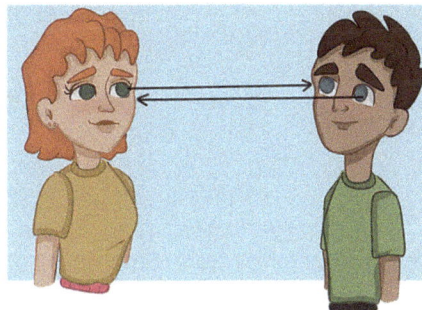

Sophia's team wants to throw the ball at the goal of Juan's team, and Juan's team wants to throw the ball at the goal of Sophia's team: they want to throw the ball at each other's goals.

THEY SEE EACH OTHER = SHE SEES HIM AND HE SEES HER

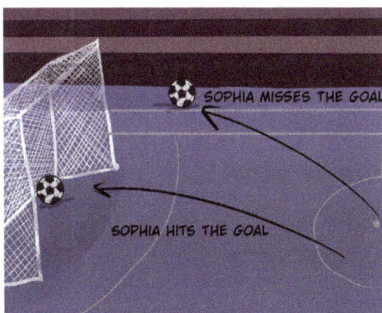

Sophia catches the ball, then throws it to Xiang. She screams: "Xiang, catch! We have to throw the ball at the goal of Juan's team!".

Sophia commands Xiang to catch the ball. Can he catch the ball? Yes, he can! Bradley screams: "Xiang, pass the ball to me!". Xiang passes the ball to Bradley. Bradley goes

then = after that (time)
I scream = I loudly say "XIANG! CATCH!"

pass (a ball) = throw it to a person in your team

SOPHIA MISSES THE GOAL

SOPHIA HITS THE GOAL

toward = to
unfortunately = sadly

Hannah sees Alessandra **go (inf.)**
pass me the ball = pass the ball to me!
order (a person to do) = command
hear = listen to
Juan hears Hannah **call (inf.)** him

I score (verb) > score (noun)
0 = zero
zero goals
zero is plural!

start = begin
ask for the ball = say: 'pass me the ball!"

move = go
left (adv.) = towards the left hand
right (adv.) = towards the right hand
right before ≠ go right

the left (noun) I **the** right (noun)
side (noun) = left or right
the left (adj.) side = the left

Team A – Team B
 1-0 Team A wins and B loses
 0-0 Draw
 0-1 Team B wins and A loses
No one ↔ all
 (= not one person)

hold hands (with a person)
 They hold each other's
 ~~hand~~ hands
 They hold hands with each other

---

toward the goal. Sophia goes too. Bradley passes the ball to Sophia. Sophia throws the ball at the goal! Unfortunately, however, Sophia misses the goal. She does not hit the goal.

Now Alessandra has the ball. She goes toward the other goal. Hannah sees Alessandra go to the other goal and says: "Alessandra, pass me the ball!". Hannah orders Alessandra to pass her the ball. Alessandra passes the ball to Hannah. Hannah sees Juan go toward the goal and says: "Juan, catch the ball!" Juan hears Hannah call him. He catches the ball. He sees Alessandra. She is close to the goal. The students of the other team are far from her. Juan passes to Alessandra, and screams: "Alessandra! Throw the ball at the goal!". Alessandra hears Juan scream. She catches the ball and throws it at the goal. She hits the goal! Now, the game's score is 1-0. Alessandra scores one goal. Juan's team has a score of one goal, and Sophia's team has a score of zero goals.

Now, Sophia starts with the ball. She sees the team go toward the goal. Jamal and Xiang ask for the ball. Each student says: "Sophia! Pass me the ball" Sophia can pass the ball to Xiang or to Jamal. Sophia decides to pass to her brother, Jamal. She sees Jamal catch the ball, and she moves toward the goal. Xiang moves toward the goal too. He asks Jamal for the ball: "Jamal! Pass me the ball!" Jamal hears Xiang ask for the ball and passes the ball to him. Xiang catches the ball. He is close to the goal. He sees the goalkeeper move left and right.

Juan can throw the ball to the left or to the right. He decides to throw to the left. Can Juan score? Yes! Juan throws the ball to the left, but the goalkeeper goes to the other side. He throws the ball to the left side, and the goalkeeper goes to the right side. Now, the game's score is 1-1. Each team has a score of one goal.

MR. MARTIN BLOWS THE WHISTLE.

Mr. Martin blows the whistle: the game is over! It is a draw: no one wins, nor loses. Mr. Martin says: "students, the game is over. You all have to go to Mrs. Williams' class!

All students hug each other and hold each other's hands. Each student hugs the other students, and each student holds hands with the other students too. Sophia hugs Bradley, Hannah, Alessandra, and so on, and she holds hands with them too. Bradley hugs Sophia, Hannah, Alessandra, and so on, and he holds hands with them too. All students hug all students and all students hold hands with the other students: they hug each other and hold each other's hands.

THEY HUG EACH OTHER.   THEY HOLD EACH OTHER'S HANDS.

Grammar

Imperative (imp.) verbs

Mr. Martin says: Sophia, **pick** the team!
Sophia says: Jamal and Xiang, **go** to the goal!
    'pick!' and **'catch!'** are **imperatives;**
Imperative verbs are always **second-person** verbs (sing. or plur.);
Imperative verbs **command, order,** or **ask for.**
Mr. Martin **commands** Sophia **to pick**: she **has to pick.**

Infinitive verbs with 'see', 'hear'… (verbs of the senses)

Jamal sees Sophia **go** to class.
Lucía hears Jamal and Juan **whisper** to the teacher.
~~I see Jamal goes to class.~~
~~I see Jamal to go to class.~~
    'go', and **'whisper'** are **infinitives.** They have **no person**.
We say infinitives with the verbs **'see', 'hear'**…
Those are **bare infinitives**.

imperative (adj.)

bare infinitive = infinitive with **no** **'to'**

THE SENSES

Exercises

How is Mr. Martin like? He is a tall, __ man. He teaches __ __. He __ (= at all times) plays in the __. The students play in the gym too. What __ do they play? They play __. When is Mr. Martin's class? It is __ after recess.

Sophia and Juan pick a team: Sophia __ Bradley: "Bradley!" Juan sees Sophia __ Bradley and calls: "Lucía!". Sophia sees Juan __ Lucía and calls: "Jamal!", and so on: Sophia and Juan call __ (= all) student to their team. Jamal __ (= listens to) Sophia call him, and goes to Sophia's __.

Sophia __ (= begin) with the ball. The team __ __ throw the ball at the goal of the other team. Bradley __ __ the ball: "Sophia, pass me the ball!" Sophia hears Bradley __ for the ball, and __ the ball to __. Can Bradley __ the ball? No! He goes __ (= to) the ball, but he cannot catch the ball. Sophia passes to Bradley, but she __ him. __ (= sadly), Bradley does not catch the ball.

Words

ask for
ball
bare infinitive
blow
call
catch
command
decide
draw
each
each other
goal
goalkeeper
gym
hand
have to (have + inf)
handball
hear
hit
hold hands
hug
imperative
left (adj.)
left (noun)
lose
miss
move
order to
pass
Physical Education (P.E.)
pick
right (adj.)
right (noun)
score (verb)
score (noun)
scream
sense (noun)
side
start
team
then
throw
toward
unfortunately
whistle
win
zero (0)

Now, Juan has the ball. He commands Lucía __ __ the ball: "Lucía! Catch the ball!". Lucía hears Juan __ her to catch the ball. Can she catch the __? Yes! She can! Lucía __ Hannah to catch the ball: "Hannah! Catch!". Hannah catches the ball. Hannah __: "ALESSANDRA! CATCH!". Alessandra hears Hannah __, and catches the ball. All students command Alessandra to __ the ball at the __: "Alessandra! __ the ball at the goal!" Alessandra throws the ball at the goal. She __ the goal! Alessandra scores. Now, the game's __ is 1-0. Juan's team has a score of one goal, and Sophia's team has a score of __ (0) __.

Sophia starts with the ball. She throws to Jamal; Jamal throws __ Bradley; Bradley throws __ Xiang. Now, Xiang is __ (↔ far from) to the goal. The __ goes __ and __. Juan can throw the ball left or right: he __ to throw the ball left. The goalkeeper __ __ (= goes to) the other __! Can Juan __? Yes! Juan __: now the game's score is 1-1. It is a __.

The game __ __ (= ends). Mr. Martin __ the __: "**preeee preeeee**" __ __ (↔ all) wins, nor __. Sophia hugs Bradley, __ (= after that) Jamal, then Xiang, then Hannah, then Alessandra, __ __ __... Hannah __ Sophia, then Bradley, and so on. All students hug __ __. The students also __ hands __ each __: Sophia holds __ with Bradley, then Lucía, then Hannah... Mr. Martin says: "students, go to Mrs. Williams' class! Now, students __ __ go to Mrs. William's class.

2.
Bradley says: "Sophia, go!". What does Bradley do?
Sophia can go left or right. What does she do?
The game is over. What does Mr. Martin do?
The game's score is 0-0. Who wins?
You are close to the goal. What do you do?
Where do the students play?
What do the students play?
When do the students play?
What grammar do we study in this chapter?
What are the two sides?

MRS. WILLIAMS

Chapter 11

Geometry

Chapter 11 Geometry

it is time for... = we have to...
old ↔ young
fat ↔ thin
fat (person) = heavy
    a fat person
    a heavy ship, book... (and a
    heavy person too)

to come = to go towards the
    speaker
    come in = come in [to the
    classroom]
    The speaker speaks = says:
    "…"

let us count = count! (imp.) and
    I count with you.
point to = point at

why...? because...

let me guess = I guess!

equal (adj.) = the same

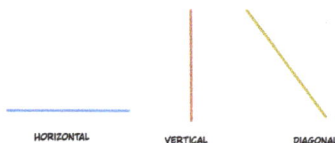

HORIZONTAL   VERTICAL   DIAGONAL

tell me = say to me
a pair = two (of the same)
1 in (inch) = 2.54 cm
    (centimeters)
look = see
measure (of a noun) = how long
    it is

A DIFFERENCE

MRS. WILLIAMS

It's time for Mrs. Williams' class! The students have to go to her class. How is Mrs. Williams like? She is an old, thin woman. She is neither young, nor fat. What does Mrs. Williams teach? She teaches geometry.

Mrs. Williams sees the students close to the classroom. She is in the classroom, and says: "Hi, students! come in!". The students are out of the classroom; they hear Mrs. Williams and joyfully go to the classroom.

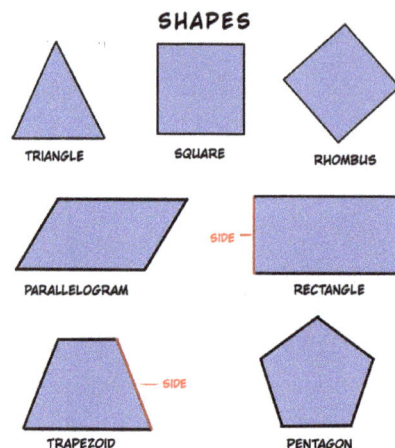

SHAPES

TRIANGLE   SQUARE   RHOMBUS

PARALLELOGRAM   SIDE   RECTANGLE

SIDE   TRAPEZOID   PENTAGON

The class begins. Mrs. Williams has many shapes. She points at a triangle and says: "What is a triangle, Juan?" Juan says: "it is a shape with three sides, Mrs. Williams." Teacher: "yes! That is correct. Here, let us count the sides: 'one…two…three…'

Mrs. Williams points to a pentagon and asks: "Hannah, what is this shape?" Hannah answers: "that is a pentagon." Teacher: "correct! Why is this shape a pentagon? Who can guess?" Sophia: "let me guess! Because it has five sides. A pentagon always has five sides". Teacher: "correct!"

The teacher points at a square and says: "what is this shape?" Jamal answers: "it is a square". Teacher: "why is it a square, Jamal?" Jamal: "because it has four sides". Teacher: "this is not completely correct. It is partially correct. A square has four sides, but how are those sides like? Let me ask another student. Lucía, can you answer?" Lucía: "A square has four sides and they are all equal. Teacher: "Yes! That is entirely correct"

The teacher points at a rectangle and says: "what is this shape?" Xiang answers: "it is a rectangle". Teacher: "why? Who can tell me?" Bradley wants to answer. He says: "let me guess! The shape is a rectangle because it has two pairs of sides, and each pair has the same measure." Teacher: "that is partially correct! Let us look at these shapes. Don't they both have two pairs of sides, and each pair has the same measure?" The teacher points at a rectangle and a parallelogram:

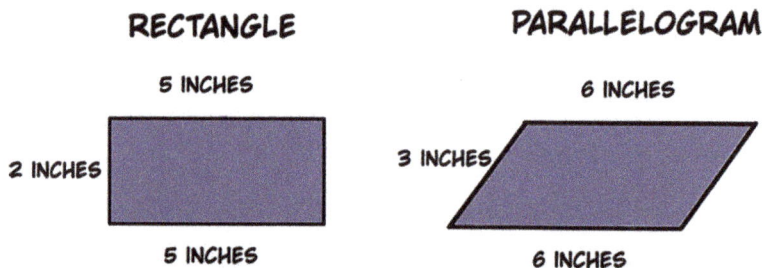

RECTANGLE

5 INCHES

2 INCHES

5 INCHES

PARALLELOGRAM

6 INCHES

3 INCHES

6 INCHES

Teacher: "the rectangle has two pairs of sides. The measure of the horizontal sides is 5 inches, and the measure of the vertical sides is 2 inches. The parallelogram has two pair of sides too. The measure of the horizontal sides is 6 inches and the measure of the diagonal sides is 3 inches. What is the difference? Let me ask you, Alessandra!"

Alessandra: "Are not the angles different?" Teacher: "yes! They are! How do they differ?" Alessandra: "the rectangle has four right angles, but the parallelogram has two acute and two obtuse angles". Teacher: "that is entirely correct, Alessandra!" Let me ask you another question: what is an acute angle?

Alessandra: it is an angle whose measure is smaller than ninety degrees (90°). Teacher: "Now, let me ask you, Juan: what is an obtuse angle?" Juan: it is an angle whose measure is greater than ninety degrees.

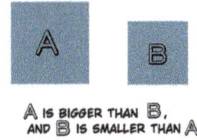

A IS BIGGER THAN B,
AND B IS SMALLER THAN A

different (adj.) < difference
I differ = I am not the same,
    I am different
smaller < small
greater < great
    great = big

```
-TY

20 TWENTY  (< TWO)
30 THIRTY  (< THREE)
40 FORTY   (< FOUR)
50 FIFTY   (< FIVE)
60 SIXTY   (< SIX)
70 SEVENTY (< SEVEN)
80 EIGHTY  (< EIGHT)
90 NINETY  (< NINE)
```

Teacher: "Those are correct answers! The measure of an acute angle is always smaller than 90°, and the measure of an obtuse angle is always greater than 90°. Tell me, Sophia, is an angle whose measure is 100° acute or obtuse?" Sophia: "It's an obtuse angle, Mrs. Williams." Teacher: "All right! Let me ask another question; what is an angle whose measure is 20°?" Lucía: "Let me answer! It is an acute angle." Teacher: "All right! And what is an angle of 40° degrees?" Jamal: "It is an acute angle too." Teacher: "Great! 10°, 20°, 30°, 40°, 50°, 60°, 70°, 80°… they are all acute angles!

100 = a hundred
all right! = That is correct!

Juan: "What about 31°? Is thirty-one degrees an acute angle too?" Teacher: "yes, Juan. An angle of thirty-one degrees is acute, so as an angle of thirty-two, thirty-three, thirty-four... degrees. Do you understand?" Juan: "Yes, I do!"

Teacher: "now, let me ask for an example of obtuse angle. Who can tell me?" Bradley: "For example, a hundred and forty-four degrees is an obtuse angle" Teacher: "All right! Now, who can tell me an angle that is neither acute nor obtuse?" Hannah: "let me answer! An angle of ninety degrees is neither acute nor obtuse." Teacher: "that is correct! What is angle of ninety degrees?" Students: "It is a right angle!" Teacher: "All right! And what about this angle of 180°?" Mrs. Williams points at the angle of 180°:

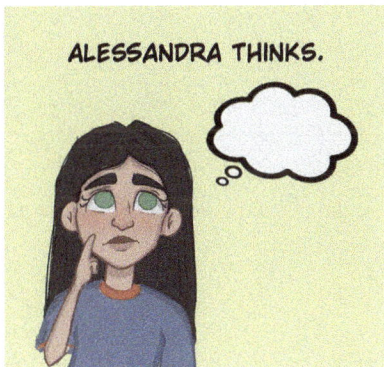

What about... (noun)?
    = I ask the same question,
    but the noun is different.
so as = same as
    so as an angle of thirty-one
    degrees [*is acute too*]
144 = a hundred and forty-four
neither...nor
    = it is not... and not...
    = it is not... nor...

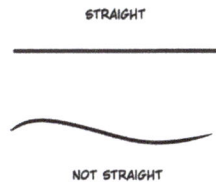

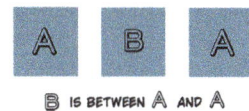

ALESSANDRA THINKS.

The students think for a long time... Alessandra: "is it not obtuse too?" Teacher: "No! We call an angle of 180° a straight angle. An obtuse angle has a measure greater than 90°, and also smaller than 180°. The measure of an obtuse angle is between ninety and a hundred and eighty degrees." Juan: "Mrs. Williams, let me ask you: what about an angle greater than 180°? For example, two hundred and thirty-two?"

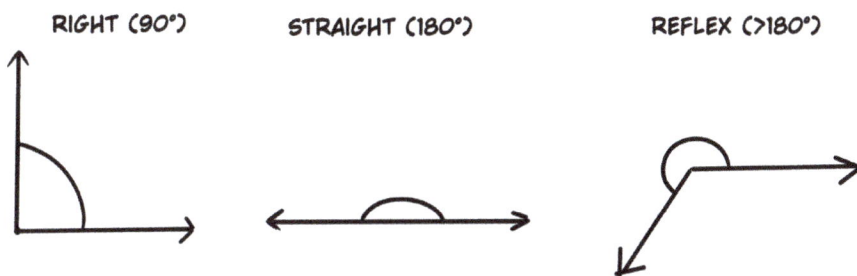

STRAIGHT

NOT STRAIGHT

B IS BETWEEN A AND A

RIGHT (90°)   STRAIGHT (180°)   REFLEX (>180°)

Mean (verb)
  ninety *means* 90
  circle *means* O

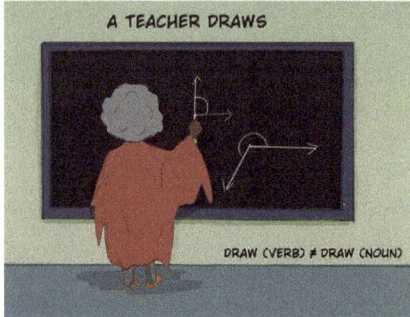

A TEACHER DRAWS

DRAW (VERB) ≠ DRAW (NOUN)

to walk *means* to go
some angles = neither all angles
    nor no angle
I add A to B = A + B = ?
    I add 10 to 2 and I have 12.
become = begin to be

Teacher: "That is a great question, Juan. We call those angles reflex angles." Juan: "why? What does reflex mean?" Teacher: "because reflex angles reflect another acute or obtuse angle. Look!" The teacher draws some angles on the blackboard:

Teacher: "The angles whose measure is greater than 180°, but smaller than 360° are reflex angles because they reflect another angle. Look! We add 70° to 290° and the angle becomes 360°; we add 160° to 200° and it becomes 360° too. Three hundred and sixty degrees is a full angle, because it is the angle of a complete circle. Do you understand?" Juan: "I do, Mrs. Williams!"

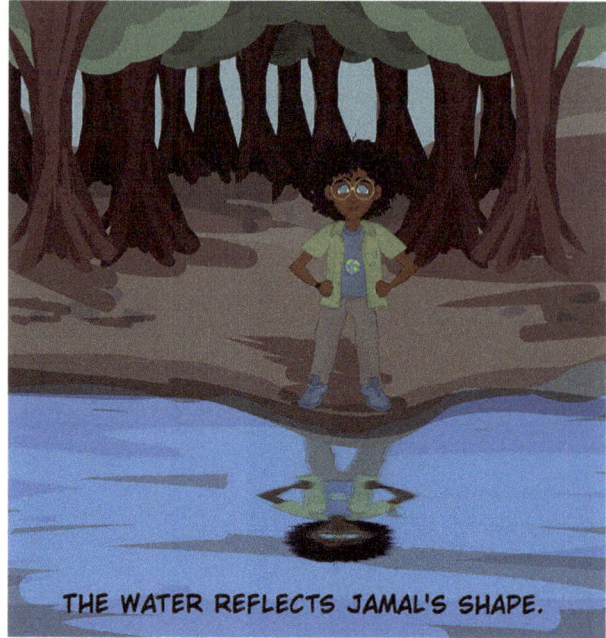

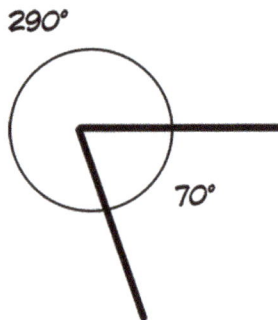

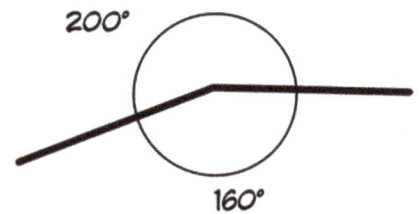

THE WATER REFLECTS JAMAL'S SHAPE.

290° 70°

200° 160°

The students draw many angles on the blackboard. Some are right angles, some are straight, some are acute, some obtuse, and some reflex. Can you draw angles too, reader? Draw some angles greater than 90°, draw some smaller! How do you call them?

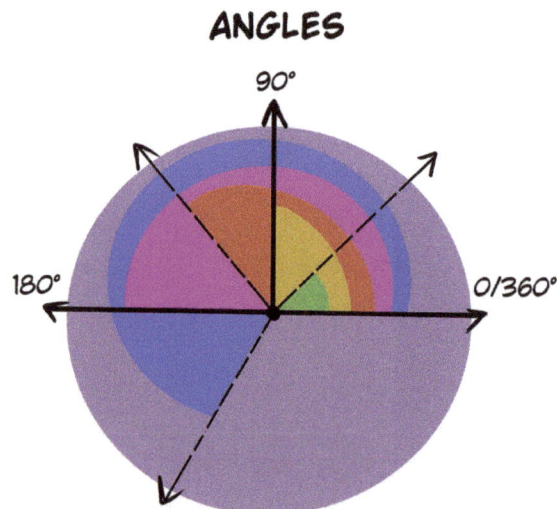

ANGLES

90°
180°
0/360°

Grammar

First-person imperative

Let me answer the question! (1ˢᵗ person singular).

Let us draw some shapes! (1ˢᵗ person plural).

There are **no first-person imperative** verb forms in English,

However, 'let me' and **'let us' mean**

the same as a first-person imperative.

'let me' is **singular (< I)**, and let us is **plural (< we)**.

Comparative adjectives

Twenty is **smaller than** twenty-one.

A hundred is **greater than** ninety-eight.

We add **-er** to an **adjective** and have its **comparative form.**

Comparative adjectives compare **two things or two people.**

We say '**than**' together with the comparative and **link** the sentences.

Exercises

1. It is time __ Ms. Williams' __. How is she like? She is an __, __ woman. An old person is not __ and a thin person is not __. What does she teach? She teaches __. She is in the classroom, and says: "students, __ in!". They hear Ms. Williams and go towards __ (= Ms. Williams). the class begins.

Ms. Williams __ many __ in the blackboard. She points at __ (= the shapes) and says: "here is a __. It has three sides. Here is a square." She asks: "Juan, __ is it a square?" Juan answers: "because it has four __". The teacher says: "this is __ correct. A __ has four sides too, but how do the square and the rectangle __ (↔ be the same)". Sophia answers: this is the __ (> differ): the square has four __ (= '=') sides, but the rectangle does not. Ms. Williams: "great! This is __ (↔ partially) correct, Sophia!" She asks Brad: "how are the sides of the rectangle?" Brad answers: "the two horizontal sides are equal, and the two __ sides are equal too." Ms. Williams: "great! What other shape has two __ (= 2) of equal sides?" Jamal answers: "the __!" Ms. Williams: "how does the parallelogram differ __ the rectangle?" Jamal: "the parallelogram has a pair of equal, horizontal sides, __ __ (= like, same as) the rectangle, and a pair of equal, __ sides.

Ms. Williams: "what __ the angles?" How are the parallelogram's angles? Alessandra: "__ me answer! It has a pair of __ and a pair of __ angles". Ms. Williams: "great! Let me ask Lucía: "what are acute and obtuse __? Lucía: "an acute angle is an angle __ measure is __ than 90 __, and an obtuse angle is an angle whose __ is __ __ 90 degrees." Ms. Williams: "great! What about the square's angles?" Juan answers: "they are all __ angles, because their measure is __ (= at all times) __ degrees. A right angle is __ (= and not) acute __ (= and not) obtuse." Ms. Williams: "great! How about an angle of 180 degrees? and of 258°?" Jamal and Sophia: let __ answer!" Ms. Williams: "O.K.!" Jamal: "the first is a __ angle." Sophia: "the second is a __ angle, Ms. Williams!"

An acute angle is always __ than a right angle. An obtuse angle is always __ than a right angle. A straight angle is always __ than a reflex angle.

I __ a right angle to an acute angle and it __ an obtuse angle. I add a straight angle __ an acute angle and it __ a __ angle.

'Smaller' and 'greater' are __ adjectives. They __ two __ or two people. I compare A and B __ I say how A and B __, or I tell the difference __ A and B.

---

form = shape

verb forms:

[I] think, [he, she, it] thinks...

[to] think

think!

comparative (adj.) < compare (verb)

I compare A and B (A and B are things)

= I say how A and B differ;

= I tell the difference between A and B.

thing ↔ person

sentence = phrase

Words

about

acute

add

angle

because

become

between

come

comparative

compare

degree

diagonal

differ

difference

different

draws

entire

equal

fat

full

geometry

great (adj.)

horizontal

hundred (100)

inch (= 2.54 cm)

let

mean

measure

neither

obtuse

old

pair

parallelogram

partial

pentagon

rectangle

reflect

Chapter 11 Geometry

reflex
right (adj.)
sentence
shape
side
so as
some
speaker
square
straight
tell
than
thin
think
thing
triangle
-ty (numbers)
vertical
why...?
young

2.
What are acute angles?
What are obtuse angles?
What are straight angles?
What are the angles whose measure is between 180 and 360 degrees?
What shape has 5 equal sides?
What is an angle of 360 degrees?
What shape has four equal, right angles?
How are the sides of the parallelogram like?
How are the sides of the rectangle like?
How is Ms. Williams like?

TABLE

DINING HALL

Chapter 12

Lunch time!

TABLE

DINING HALL

Mrs. Williams' class is over. It is time for lunch! She says goodbye to students, and holds their hands as they go to the dining hall. What time is it? It is 1 p.m. The students begin to study at 9 a.m. and finish at 1 p.m.

goodbye ↔ hi
as = at the same time
to finish = to be over
a.m. p.m.
    a.m. = before 12 o'clock
    p.m. = after 12 o'clock

Of course = **yes!!!**
Come here = come to me!

WHITE CANE

SERVICE DOG

There, the students see Fatima. They say: "Hi, Fatima! Do you want to sit with us?" Fatima hears the students ask her to sit with them, and says: "Of course! Is there a chair for Cor-kun too?" Jamal: "Yes, of course there is a chair for it! Come here!" Jamal calls Fatima and Cor-kun to the table.

Cor-kun is a service dog. It helps Fatima walk. She is blind, so she can't see. Cor-kun walks with Fatima to help her. Fatima's white cane also helps her walk. She holds the cane as she walks with Cor-kun.

can't = cannot
So (conj.)
    why can't Fatima see?
    Because she is blind.
    = Fatima is blind, **so** she
    cannot see.
by (prep.) = close to
happy ↔ sad

have lunch = eat (between
    12 o'clock and 3 p.m.)
    talk about X = say: X is...

THE PERSON EATS.

NOM NOM

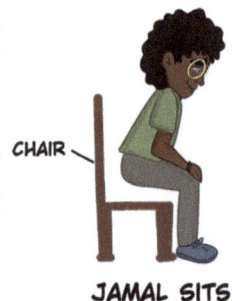

CHAIR

JAMAL SITS.

There are four chairs by the table, so four students can sit by it: Jamal, Sophia, Bradley, and Fatima. The students happily have lunch. What do they say to each other? They talk about classes, about the teachers, about their family and relatives.

kind
    potato, rice, chicken,
    tomato... are *kinds* of food
    green, yellow, red...
    are *kinds* of colors

They also talk about food. Each student eats a different kind of food: Jamal and Sophia eat pasta with tomato sauce, Bradley eats potatoes and Brussel sprouts, and Fatima eats rice and chicken.

Whose food is the rice and chicken? It's Fatima's. She eats rice and chicken. Is the rice and chicken Sophia's food too? No, hers is pasta with tomato sauce. Is Bradley's food rice and chicken? No, his is potatoes and Brussel sprouts. Who eats pasta with tomato sauce? Jamal and Sophia do.

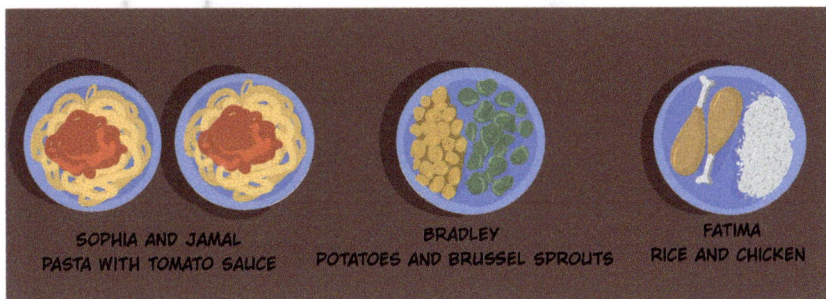

SOPHIA AND JAMAL
PASTA WITH TOMATO SAUCE

BRADLEY
POTATOES AND BRUSSEL SPROUTS

FATIMA
RICE AND CHICKEN

Bradley says: "nom nom! This food is good. Do you want to eat some, Fatima?" Fatima: "Thank you! Yes, I do, Bradley." Fatima eats some potatoes and Brussel sprouts, and says: "nom nom! Your food is good! Do you want to eat some of mine too, Bradley? My food is rice and chicken." Bradley tries some rice and chicken and says: "my food is good, but yours is better, Fatima! It is great! Thank you"

Sophia and Jamal say: "you all, eat some of our food too! Ours is pasta with tomato sauce." Fatima and Bradley eat some pasta. She says to Bradley: "I like your food, Bradley, but theirs is better! Jamal and Sophia's food is better than yours and better than mine!"

While the students talk about food, Cor-kun drools. It is hungry too! Does it eat rice and chicken with Fatima? No, it has a food of its own. Cor-kun eats dog food! While Cor-kun works, however, it doesn't eat.

COR-KUN DROOLS.

The students finish lunch, so they start to talk about other things. They talk about recess, about Mrs. Williams' class, and about tests. As they talk about those, Jamal says: "My grades are great! They are better than yours, Sophia!" Sophia is angry. She begins to talk about her own grades: "Mine are great too! Better than yours! About his own grades, Bradley adds: "my grades are not bad either!"

A SMART PERSON Fatima: "I do well on tests too, but to do well is not to be smart. Some people do better, and some people do worse. Why are we angry at each other? Jamal: You are right, Fatima... I don't want to be angry." Sophia: "neither do I!

GRADES

TEST D

TEST C⁻

TEST B⁺

TEST A⁺

WORSE

BAD

GOOD

BETTER

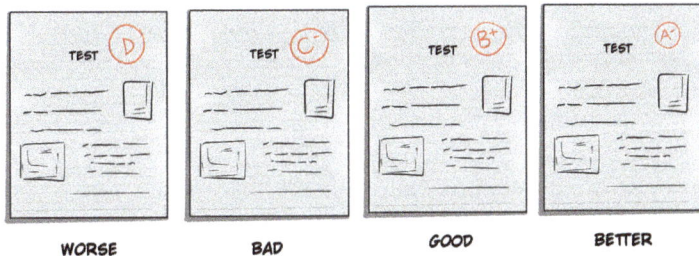

Fatima: "great! I can tell you all a story about three smart old men... They do not talk about grades, but each wants to be better than the other two. Do you all want to hear it?" Students: "yes, Fatima! We like to hear your stories!

---

hers (possessive pron.) = her food
his (pos. pron..) = his food
good = great

A CHICKEN

A TOMATO

TOMATO SAUCE

A POTATO

Thank you! = I am happy because you say...

mine (pos. pron.) = my food
yours (pos. pron.) = your food
better (comp.) < good

ours (pos. pron.) = our food
theirs (pos. pron.) = their (Jamal and Sophia's) food

to be hungry = to want to eat
    of its *own* (pos. **adj**.) = of its own *kind*
    of its *own* kind = of *the dog* kind
    there is no pos. pron. for "it"
work = have an occupation

bad ↔ good
adds *words to the sentence*
my grades are not bad either
    = neither are my grades bad

well (adv.) < good
worse ↔ better
right (adj.) = correct

SOPHIA IS ANGRY

story
    each chapter in this book tells a story

I like to = I am happy to...
wife (relation)
    Mrs. Johnson is the wife of Mr. Anderson

Fatima: "great! I am happy to tell the stories too, so sit and listen! It starts with King Shahryar and his wife, the Queen..."

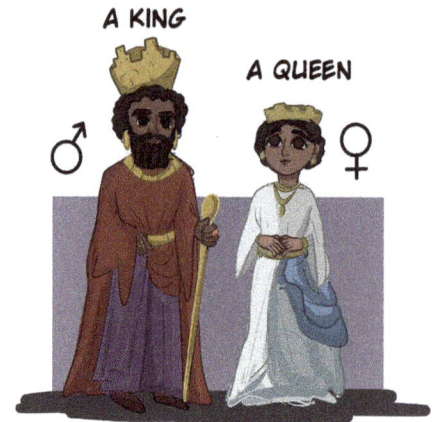

A KING ♂ A QUEEN ♀

Grammar

Possesive Pronouns (pos. pron.)

Sophia eats big potatoes and Jamal eats small potatoes:
hers are big and **his** are small.
(hers = her potatoes; his = his potatoes)

Hey! These books are **mine!**
(mine = my books)

Juan and Lucía say: "we eat at a small table and you all eat at a big table:
ours is small and **yours** is big."
(our = our table, yours = your table)

Juan and Lucía eat at a small table, and you eat at a big table: **theirs** is small, but **yours** is big.
(theirs = their table, yours = your table)
'mine', 'yours', 'his', 'hers', 'our', 'yours', 'theirs' are **possessive pronouns;**
Possessive pronoun = possessive adjective + noun;
'it' has **no possessive pronoun**:
We say: "hey! That food is **the dog's** [food]." **or** "hey! That food is **its food**."
we **don't say**: "hey! That food is ~~its~~"

Words

Cor-kun
Fatima
king
lunch
ours
queen
thank you!
angry
bad
better
blind
Brussel sprouts
by
white cane
chair
chicken
of course!
dining hall
drool
either
finish
food
good
goodbye
grade
happy

PERSONAL PRONOUN	POSSESSIVE ADJECTIVE	POSSESSIVE PRONOUN
I	MY	MINE
YOU	YOUR	YOURS
HE/SHE/IT	HIS/HER/ITS	HIS/HERS/XX
WE	OUR	OURS
YOU ALL	YOURS	YOURS
THEY	THEIR	THEIRS

Exercises

Mrs. Williams' class ___ (= is over). The students say ___ (↔ hi!) to ___ (= Mrs. Williams). What time is it? It is 1 o'clock. Is it 1 ___ (= after 12:00) or ___ (= before 12:00). It is 1 o'clock p.m. Mrs. Williams's class is over ___ 1 p.m. It is time for ___! The students go to the ___ ___.

Fatima and Cor-Kun are ___ (= in the dining hall). What is Cor-Kun? It is a ___ dog. It ___ Fatima walk. The ___ ___ also helps Fatima walk. They help Fatima walk because she is ___, so she ___ (= cannot) see. The students sit, and say: "Fatima, do you ___ to sit with ___?" Fatima hears the students ___ ___ to sit with ___ and says: "___ ___! (= yes!!!)"

There are four chairs ___ the ___, so four students can sit by it. They ___ (↔sadly) eat and talk ___ food. Each eats a different ___ ___ food. Jamal and Sophia eat ___ with ___ sauce. They say: "we ___ (= are happy to) to eat this food: ___ (= our food) is pasta with tomato ___. Fatima eats ___ and ___. She says: "I like to eat ___ (= my food) too! Do you like to eat ___ (= your food), Bradley?" Bradley answers: "yes, I do! I eat ___ and ___ ___".

Fatima and Bradley like their food. __ (= Fatima's) is rice and chicken, and __ (=Bradley's) is potatoes and Brussel sprouts. Sophia and Jamal like their food too. __ (= Jamal's and Sophia's) is pasta with tomato sauce. Is Cor-kun's food pasta with tomato sauce too? No, __ __ (= the dog's food) is different! It has a food of __ __. Kor-kun is __ (= wants to eat). It __. However, when Cor-kun __, he does not eat.

The students talk about __ too. Bradley says: "I have good grades: I do __ on __." Sophia says: "I have __ __ too: B grades and B+ grades!" Jamal says: "I have __ grades: "A grades and A+ grades! My grades are better than __, Sophia! B grades are __ than A grades." Sophia is __: "B+ is good and B is not __ __ (= also not not good)!" Fatima: "Don't be angry! I do well too, but to do well is not to __ __. Let __ (= the students) talk about another thing! Do you all want to hear a __? It is about __ Sharyar and his wife, the __."

2.
What is Cor-kun?
Why does Cor-kun help Fatima?
What else helps Fatima?
Where are the students?
What grade is better: B or A?
What grade is worse: F or B?
What do the children eat?
Whose food are the Brussel sprouts?
Whose is the pasta with tomato sauce?
Who is the wife of the king?
When do people have lunch?
Do you do well on tests?

help
hers
hungry
kind
like (verb.)
mine
own
pasta
potato
rice
tomato sauce
service dog
Shahryar
smart
so
story
test
well
wife
works
worse
yours

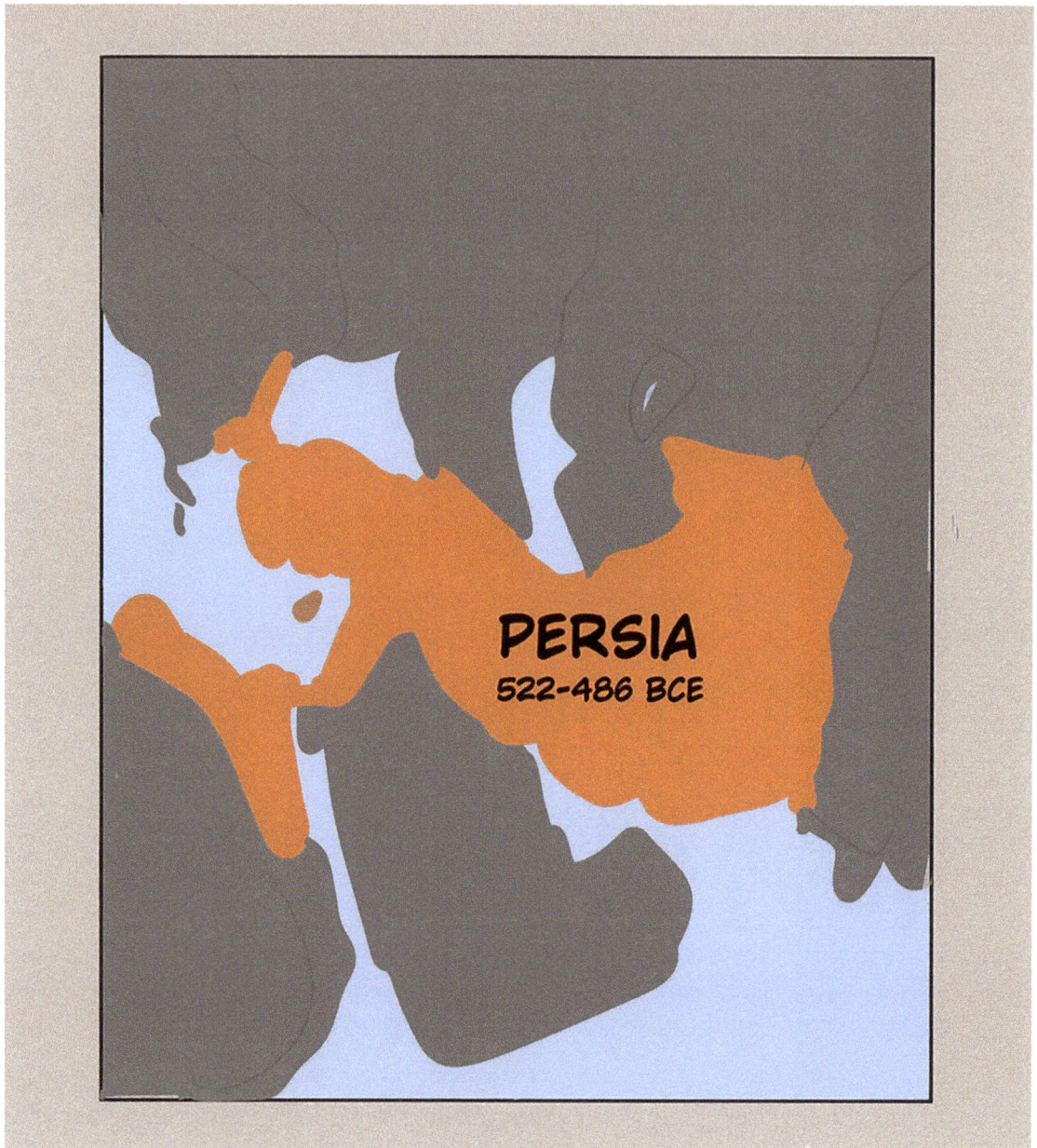

PERSIA
522-486 BCE

Chapter 13

Scheherazade

Fatima begins to tell the story. She talks about the past. The past is not now, but before now! The past was…

Fatima: "a long time ago, there was a man. His name was Shahryar. He was the king of Persia. He had a wife. She was a young woman, but her eyes were old and sad, because she did not like the king as the king liked her.

Shahryar loved her, but she did not love him. She loved another man. The king was not happy to hear about the queen's love. When he did, he became angry! His eyes became two fire balls, angry because his love did not love him. So, the king decided to kill the queen: He commanded someone to kill her. So, the queen was not alive: she was dead.

Shahryar then commanded another woman to become his wife for one day and one night. After one day and one night he commanded someone to kill her too, and the wife lived not: she died. For many days and many nights, the king commanded a woman to become his wife, then commanded someone to kill the same woman after one day and one night.

THE MAN KILLS THE QUEEN

Soon, the king could not kill other women. There were few women alive in Persia. Many died because of the king's commands. However, Scheherazade lived. She was the daughter of the vizier. The vizier helped the king decide, when the king wanted someone to help. The vizier did not want Scheherazade to become the king's wife, however, because he did not want her to die.

THE NIGHT (⟷ DAY)

SCHEHERAZADE AND VIZIER

Scheherazade said: "Father, let me become the king's wife. I can do something to help! As water extinguishes the fire, I can do something to make the king stop. The vizier answered: "but, daughter! How can you make the king stop? He killed each one of his wives. He can kill you too! I do not want you to die, my good daughter!" Scheherazade answered: "How? With stories. Can I not tell many stories, father?""

Fatima stopped for a little time and started again: "So, Scheherazade became the king's wife. After one day, before it became night, she said: "King Shahryar, do you want to hear a story…?" The king was curious. He said: "a story, you say? What is your story about?". Scheherazade started to narrate a story, but when the night ended and it became day, she stopped, and said: "I want to sleep". The king answered: "but the story did not end! I am curious about how it ends!". Schererazade, however, slept. The day after, the king did not kill her. He could not, because he was curious about the story. So on the next night Scheherazade continued to tell it, and on the next, and on the

SHEHERAZADE SLEEPS

---

the past *time* = time before now
is (now), was (past)
name = the word that means a person
ago (adv.) = before now
have (now), had (past)
are (now), were (past)
did (past) < do
    she likes the king (now)
    she **did** not **like** (*inf.*) the king (past negative)
like (now), like**d** (past)
love = I like much ❤️
hear (now), hear**d** (past)
become (now), became (past)
decide, decide**d**
command, commande**d**

someone = some person
    one = a person
I live = I am alive
    ↔ I die = I am dead
many (countable) = much (uncountable)

soon = after not much time
can (now), could (past)
few (count.) ↔ many (count.)
help, help**ed**
want, want**ed**

say, sai**d**
    something = some thing
I make someone + inf
    water makes the fire die
stop = end, not go
wives (plur.) < wife (sing.)

again (adv.) = another time
curious (adj.)
    a curious person wants to hear about something
narrate, narrate**d** = tell

sleep (*now*), slept (past)

Chapter 13 Scheherazade

can (now), could (past)
next (adv.) = right after
continue, continued ↔ stop
a thousand = 1000
    a thousand and one = 1001

regular = always the same
    help, helped I narrate,
    narrated I like, liked I want,
    wanted I live, lived I love,
    loved...

irregular ↔ regular
    am, **was** I is **was** I are **were** I
    have **had** I become **became** I
    do **did**... I can, **could**

negate a verb = make the verb
be negative

an exception
    = an example different from
    the regular examples.

Words
again
ago
alive
answer, ed
become, became
continue, ed
can, could
curious
day
dead
decide, ed
do, did
die, ed
-[e]d
exception
few
form
have, had
irregular
kill, ed
like, ed
live, ed
love, ed
make, made
name
narrate, ed
negate, ed

next… and so on for a thousand and one nights... And after four hundred and fourteen nights, Scheherazade started to tell the story about three men. Do you want to hear it?" Students: "yes! We are curious!"

Grammar
Simple Past
    Shahryar **was** the king of Persia.
    Fatima decide**d** to tell a story during lunch time.
    The teacher command**ed** the students to go to class.
    Fatima stop**ped** for a little time.
        The **simple past** says something about the **time before now**.
      We add **-d** or **-ed** to a verb to form the **regular** simple past.
        Some verbs have **irregular forms.**

Simple Past – negative
    Xiang **did** (< do) *not* **pass** (infinitive) the ball.
    Jessica **did** *not* **go** to class.
    Scheherazade **was not** the queen of Persia.

    We **negate** the simple past of a verb with 'did' + **infinitive** of the verb;
        '**Did**' is the **past form** of '**do**';
        the linking verb '**to be**' is **an exception:**
    We **do not** say "Scheherazade ~~did not be~~ the queen of Persia".

Exercises
1. Fatima talks about the __. The past __ (< is) before now.
Fatima: "a long time __, Shahryar was the king of __. He __ (< have) a __ (↔ husband), who was a __ (↔ old) woman, but whose eyes __ (< are) old and __ (↔ happy), because she __ not __ (= like much) the king like the king __ her.

She loved __ (= not the king) man. When the king __ (< hear) about this man, he __ (< become) __! His eyes became two __ __, so he __ to __ (= make not alive) the queen. He said to __ (a person): kill the queen! I __ you to kill her!" So, the queen __ (= became dead).

__ (= after that time), Shahryar commanded another woman to become his wife __ one __ and one __. After this time, he __ someone to __ __ (= the woman) too! The many __ (= wife, plur.) of the king did not __ (= be alive).

__ (= not a long time after), the king __ (< can) not kill other __ (= woman, plur.), because __ (= not many) were __ (↔ dead) in Persia. Scheherazade, however, the daughter of the __, __ (< want) to help. She said: "__ (a person) __ (< have) to stop the king! As water __ (= makes the fire die) the fire, I can do __ (a thing) to help!" The Vizier, however, __ not __ (< want) his daughter to __ the king's __.

Scheherazade, however, __ not __ (< die), because she __ (< narrate)__ to the king. When night __ (< come), Scheherazade __ (< begin) to __ (= narrate) a story. Before night was __ (= ended), however, she __ (< stop) and __ (< sleep). The king was __, but Scheherazade __ not tell him the end of the story. The day __, the king __ not __ (< kill) her. And so on, for __ (1000) and one nights.

'Answered', 'continued', 'killed', 'loved' are all __ verbs. They have regular __ in the __ past. 'Became', '__' (< can), '__' (< have), '__' (< do), '__' (< is), and '__' (< are) are all __ verbs. They have __ forms in the simple past.

The verb 'did' also __ (= makes negative) the simple past form of the verbs. It does not negate, however, the verb __. This verb is an __.
2.

Chapter 13 Scheherazade

Who was Scheherazade?
Whose daughter was Scheherazade?
Who was Sharyar?
Where was Sharyar king?
How did Scheherazade not die?
Was the king's wife happy?
How were the queen's eyes like?
What are irregular verbs?
Can you tell examples of irregular verbs?
How do we negate the simple past of a verb?
How do we negate the verb 'to be'?

next
night
past
Persia
regular
say, said
Scheherazade
simple
sing, ed
sleep, slept
someone
something
soon
start, ed
stop, stopped
talk, ed
thousand (1000)
vizier
want, ed
is, was
are, were

BYZANTINE   PERSIAN   INDIAN

BYZANTIUM   PERSIA   INDIA

Chapter 14

The Three Wise Men

Chapter 14 The Three Wise Men

BYZANTIUM PERSIA INDIA

wise = very smart

VERY (ADV.) [+ ADJ. OR ADV.]

A VERY TALL GIRL

A TALL GIRL

A SHORT GIRL

The students were very curious, so Fatima began her story again: "a long time ago, there was a king, whose name was Sabur. He was Persian just as king Sharyar, whose story I just told. Sabur was a king who had much money, so he was very rich. Are not people who have much money rich? He was a king whom everyone loved, and to whom many people came every day and every night. They asked for food, and the king gave food to them;

begin, began (past)
just (adv.) as = entirely the same as
just (adv.) = right before now
tell, told (past)
everyone = all the people
    every (3+) = each (2+)
come, came (past)
    come to someone = go towards someone [and ask for something]

they asked for money, and the king gave money to them; they asked for a story, and the king told a story to them. Whoever came to the king received something. He gave whatever people asked for to whomever asked for it. He was a very generous king."

Jamal asks: "Fatima, did king Sabur live at the same time when king Shahryar lived?" Fatima answers: "No, Jamal, king Sabur lived before king Shahryar. Sabur died before Shahryar became king." Lucía asks: "why did king Sabur give so much to whomever asked?" Fatima answers: "He was very rich, and it made him happy to give whatever people asked for."

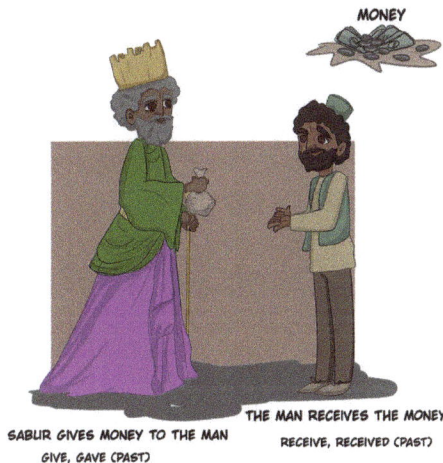

MONEY

SABUR GIVES MONEY TO THE MAN
GIVE, GAVE (PAST)

THE MAN RECEIVES THE MONEY
RECEIVE, RECEIVED (PAST)

whoever came received... =
    = all who came received...
he gave to whomever came =
    = he gave to all who came
whatever (thing) ≠ whoever (person)
generous (adj.) = who gives much

so much = this very much
make, made
it made him happy to give
    = he became happy when he gave

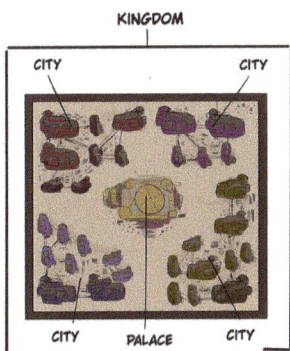

KINGDOM

CITY   CITY

CITY PALACE CITY

Fatima continues to narrate: "so, king Sabur was very generous. He also liked to study, so he often called wise men and women to the palace. They came from all places: from other kingdoms and from cities all over Sabur's kingdom, sometimes from close cities, some other times from cities far from the palace.

place = where something is
all over = in all places

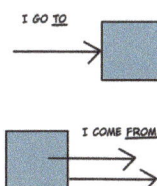

I GO TO

I COME FROM

NEVER SELDOM SOMETIMES OFTEN ALWAYS

65

to bring = to have and go with
the wise man brings a gift
from India
gift = every thing we give

So three wise men came to the palace, an Indian, a Byzantine, and a Persian, from Sabur's own kingdom. The king asked: "who are you all, whom I see? Why did you all come to my palace?"

The first man answered: "O, generous king, I come from India, and I bring a gift: this statue. It holds a trumpet, so it can loudly sound when an enemy comes

THE TRUMPET SOUNDS:
STATUE   TRUMPET
ENEMY

may = can (sometimes!)
I may
husband (relation)
Mr. Anderson is the husband
of Mrs. Johnson

The king said: "this is a great gift! This Indian man whom I see is wise, this man whose gift I now possess." The king asked the Indian wise man: "tell me, O wise man, what do you want from me? What gift may I give to you?"

The man answered: "the question, o generous king, is not what, but whom you may give to me, because I want your daughter. She is the person whom I want, so we can become husband and wife. The king answered: "As Allah lives, may my first daughter become your wife!"

As Allah lives = because Allah is alive
may...! = let! (sometimes!)
She may (not she ~~mays~~)

Then came the man whom we call Byzantine, and whom the Persians called Rumi (because 'Rumi', in Persian, means 'Byzantine' in English). He said: "O, generous king, I come from Byzantium, and I bring a gift: this peacock, and its twenty-four peahens. It shows the time; each peahen is an hour, and the peacock points at each peahen when the right hour comes. When it is 1:00, the peacock points at the first peahen; when it is 2:00, it points at the second peahen, and so on…"

PEACOCK ♂
PEAHEN ♀

I show = I make someone see, I point at
hour
1:00, 2:00, 3:00... are hours.

The king said: "this is a great gift! This Rumi man whom I see is wise, this man whose gift I now possess." The king asked the wise man: "tell me, O wise man, what do you want from me? What gift may I give to you?"

The Byzantine answered: "the question, o generous king, is not what, but whom you may give to me, because I want your daughter. She is the person whom I want, so we can become husband and wife. The king answered: "As Allah lives, may my second daughter become your wife!"

THE HORSE TRAVELS BETWEEN CITIES
CITIES
THE EBONY (=BLACK) HORSE

as well = too, also
I travel = I go far (to another
city, kingdom...)
a year = 365 days
not only...but also = and...and...
< only (adv. < one)

Then came the Persian man, from Sabur's own kingdom. He said: "o generous king. As I love you, my king, may you love my gift as well! I come from your own kingdom, and bring this gift: an ebony horse. It can travel in one day the same as other horses can travel in a year!"

The king said: "this is a great gift! This man whom I see is not only a good Persian, but also very wise, this man whose gift I now possess." The king asked the wise man: "tell me, O wise man, what do you want from me? What gift may I give to you?"

The Byzantine answered: "the question, o compatriot king, is not what, but whom you may give to me, because I want your daughter. She is the person whom I want, so we can become husband and wife. The king answered: "As Allah lives, may my third daughter become your wife!"

Brad is very curious. He interrupts Fatima: "Fatima, I want to hear what the king did! Did he give his daughters to the wise men? Did the daughters marry the wise men?

Grammar
Modal Verbs

Can *Fatima* **tell** a story?
Teacher: "*Bradley* **may go**, but *Jamal* **may not [go]**."
May *Sophia* and *Jamal* **be** well!
Modal verbs *modify* **another verb.**
This verb is an **infinitive:** we say: "may Sophia **be** well",
NOT "may Sophia ~~is~~ well"
Modal verbs have **no infinitive** and **do not change.**
We **do not say:** "I want ~~to may~~". We say: "**may I!**"

Simple Past – Interrogative
Did Shahryar **kill** the queen? Yes, he did.
Could Shahryar **kill** the queen? No, he **could** not.
Were the three men wise? Yes, they were.

We ask questions in the simple past with **'did' + the infinitive** of the verb;
Modal verbs are **exceptions,** because they **don't have infinitives:**
We **do not** say: "did Shahryar ~~can~~ kill the queen"
The linking verb **'to be'** is **an exception too.**
We **do not say "~~did Sabur be~~** king of Persia?".

Relative Pronouns
Who is Jamal? **He** is Sophia's brother.
Jamal is the boy **who** is *Sophia's* brother.

Whose brother is Jamal? He is **Sophia's** brother.
Sophia is the girl **whose** brother is *Jamal*

Whom does Sophia see? She sees **Jamal.**
Jamal is the boy **whom** *Sophia* sees.

To whom does Jamal throw the ball? He throws the ball **to Sophia.**
Sophia is the girl **to whom** *Jamal* throws the ball.

Relative pronouns change; we say…
'who' when we talk about the **subject** of a sentence;
'whose' when we talk about **a person who has / possesses a thing;**
'whom' when we talk about the **object** of a **verb;**
'preposition + whom' when we talk about the **object** of a **preposition.**
Relative pronouns can be interrogative too.

Exercises
Fatima __ (< begin) the story__ (= another time). It was about a __ king, __ name was Sabur, and three __ men, one of __ was an __, the other __, and the third a Persian, from Sabur's __ __. The king had much __, so he was very __, and __ (< give) __ to __ asked. He was a king __ everyone loved, and to __ many __ (< come) __ (= each) day and __ night. __ came to the king __ (↔ gave) something. The king gave __ people asked for to __ asked for it…"

---

compatriot (adj.)
A Persian and a Persian are compatriots;
A Rumi and a Rumi are compatriots;
A Persian and a Rumi are not.

I Interrupt = I say something while someone else speaks.
I marry = I become a husband / wife
later (adv.) = after now

Modal verbs don't change: I **can,** you **can,** he **can,** she **can,** it **can,** we **can,** you all **can,** they **can**...

SUBJECT	WHO
POSSESSIVE	WHOSE
OBJECT OF THE VERB	WHOM
OBJECT OF PREPOSITION	TO WHOM, WITH WHOM, TOWARDS WHOM, OF WHOM...

Chapter 14 The Three Wise Men

Words

affirmative
Allah
begin, began
bring
Byzantine
come, came
city
compatriot
ebony
enemy
-ever
every
everyone
give, gave
generous
gift
horse
hour
husband
India
Indian
interrupt
just (adv.)
kingdom
later
make, made
marry, ied
may
modal
money
often
only
palace
peacock
peahen
place
receive, ed
rich
Rumi
Sabur
show, ed
sometimes
sound, ed
statue
tell, told
travel, led
trumpet
very
whatever
whoever
whomever
wise

Jamal __ Fatima: "Fatima, __ Sabur __ at the same time when Shahryar lived?" Fatima answers: "no, Sabur lived __ Shahryar. She __ to __: "king Sabur also liked to __, so he __ (more than sometimes) called wise men from other __ and __ all __ Persia. __ (= neither always nor never) he wise men came from close cities, __ other times they __ (< come) __ cities far __ from the __ (= king's house)."

When the wise men came to the palace, Sabur asked: "__ are you all, __ come to my palace, and __ I see __ (= have and go with) gifts to me?" So __ (= each) man __ (< answer) the king. The first, who was __, said: "I bring a __. It __ a trumpet when the __ comes. The second, __ was __, said: "I bring a __ and __ (= 24) __. The peacock points at __ peahen when the right __ comes. The third, __ __ Persian, __: "I bring an __ (= black) __. It can __ in one __ the same __ other horses __ travel in a __.

The king __ (= like very much) every gift, and said: "Now I want to give a __ to __ gave me a gift." So, he asked each wise man: "O, wise man, __ gift I now possess, and __ I see is very smart, what gift do you want from me? What gift __ I give you? Each wise man, however, answered: "the __ is not __, but __ you may give me, king, because I __ your __. she is the person __ I want, so we __ become __ and wife." To each wise man the king answered: "as __ __, may my daughter become your wife!"

'Can' and 'may' are __ verbs. They do not have an __, and they do not __: we say: "I may, you __, he __, she __, it __, we __, you all __, and they __.

Modal verbs __ another verb, whose form is the infinitive. We say: "may king Sabur __ for a long time!" We also say: "may Sophia __ (< am, is, are) well!".

We ask questions in the simple past with __ + the __ of the verb. For example: "__ Scheherazade __ (< die, died)? Modal verbs, however, are an __. We say: "__ (< can) Scheherazade stop the king? The verb 'to be' is an exception too. We say: "__ Sabur the king of Persia?".

Relative pronouns can be __ or __. For example: the sentence "Who was Sabur?" has an __ pronoun, and the sentence "Sabur was the king about whom I heard" has an __ pronoun.

2.

What gift did the Indian give to the king?
What did this gift do?
What about the Rumi?
What did the Rumi's gift do?
What about the Persian?
What did the Persian's gift do?
Who was Sabur?
Did Sabur and Shahryar lived at the same time?
Where was Sabur king?
What did Sabut give to people?
Whom did the wise men ask from the king?
What did the king answer to the wise men?

Chapter 15

The Ebony Horse

Chapter 15 The Ebony Horse

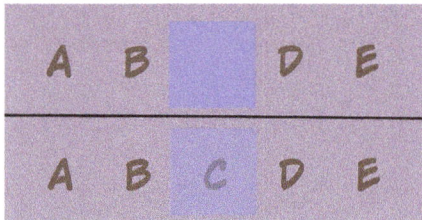

A B [ ] D E

A B C D E

C IS BEHIND THE SQUARE

CURTAIN

speak, spoke
everything = every thing, each thing

wear, wore = have clothes
much < more < most
little < less < least
adj. + -est
    long < longer < longest
    short < shorter < shortest

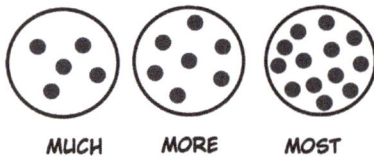

MUCH   MORE   MOST

seach of whom he gave to
    = he gave each of them to...
old < older < oldest
young < younger < youngest

Fatima begins to tell the story again: "While the king and the wise men spoke about the marriage, the three daughters heard everything, because they were behind a curtain.

All three daughters had long hair, and wore colorful clothes. The first had much hair and wore a blue tunic. The second had more hair, and wore a more colorful tunic: it was blue and green. The third had the most hair, and wore the most colorful tunic: it was blue, green, yellow, and purple! The third daughter, whose hair was the longest, had the most hair. The first daughter, whose hair was the shortest, had the least hair. The second daughter had more hair than the first, but less hair than the third.

LONG   LONGER   LONGEST
TUNIC   CLOTHES   PURPLE
COLORFUL   MORE COLORFUL   MOST COLORFUL

The king had three daughters, each of whom he gave to one of the wise men: He gave the first, who was also the oldest, to the Indian. He gave the second, who was neither the oldest nor the youngest, to the Rumi. He gave the third, who was the youngest, to the Persian.

The Indian, however, to whom the king gave the oldest daughter, was the youngest of the wise men. The Persian, to whom the king gave the youngest daughter, was the oldest of the wise men. Only the Rumi, to whom the king gave the daughter who was neither the oldest nor the youngest, was also neither the youngest nor the oldest.

Chapter 15 The Ebony Horse

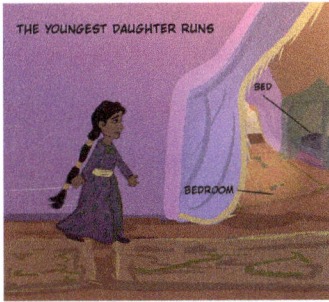
THE YOUNGEST DAUGHTER RUNS

So, the youngest daughter became furious! She ran to her bedroom, and screamed: "Oh! Why?! Why?! Why did my father give me, his youngest daughter, to the oldest wise man?! I don't want to marry him!"

While she screamed, the Princess tore her clothes (in Persia people tore their own clothes when they were very angry). Her brother, the Prince, saw the Princess tear her clothes, and came to her. He said: "O, sister, why are you so angry? What makes you so sad? The princess answered: "our father, oh brother, our father wants to give me in marriage to the oldest wise man who came to the palace." The prince said: "do not be sad!", and he went to the king's palace, because he wanted to talk to his father.

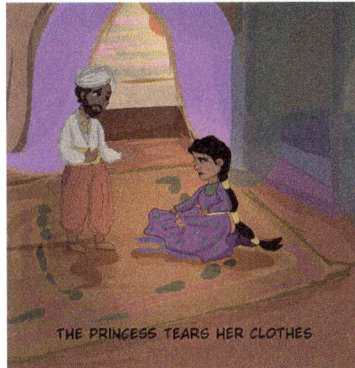
THE PRINCESS TEARS HER CLOTHES

There, the prince said: "father, why do you want to give my youngest sister to this man whom I see, who is the oldest of these three?" The king answered: "I want to give my youngest daughter to him because he gave the best gift to me. Look! He gave me this ebony horse. It can travel in one day the same as other horses travel in a year!"

THE PRINCE RIDES THE EBONY HORSE

The prince was curious to see the horse, because it was the best horse in the kingdom. He asked the Persian wise man: "teach me how to ride this horse!"

So, the Persian came towards the prince and the horse, and said: "look at this mechanism: it makes the horse go up". The prince, however, interrupted the wise man: "great!". He pulled the mechanism up. The horse went up, and higher, and so on, until it came to the highest sky.

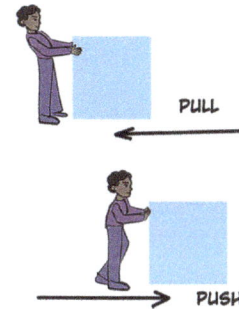

ssfurious = very angry
run, ran

tear, tore

Princess = daughter of the king
　　Prince = son of the king
see, saw
so sad = very sad

go, went

good < better < best
He gave me this horse
　　= he gave this horse to me

PULL
PUSH

curious (+inf)

until (adv.) = to the time when

Chapter 15 The Ebony Horse

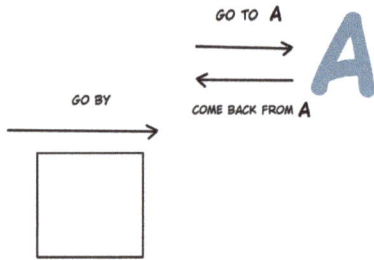

GO TO A

GO BY

COME BACK FROM A

A

didn't = did not
go away = go far from the speaker
teach, taught

think, thought
bad < worse < worst
dumb ↔ wise

DIRTY   **NOT DIRTY**

as = while

can, could
however much he wanted *to breathe*
   = but he wanted to breath much
can't = cannot

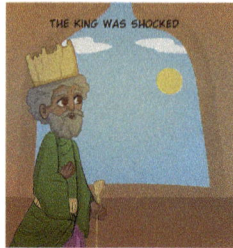

THE KING WAS SHOCKED

When the king saw the horse go up so high, he was shocked! The Prince, however, did not come back. The first (1st) hour went by, then the second (2nd), then the third (3rd), then the fourth (4th), then the fifth (5th), the sixth (6th), the seventh (7th), the eighth (8th), the ninth (9th), the tenth (10th), the eleventh (11th), the twelfth (12th), the thirteenth (13th)...

THE KING WAS WORRIED

It became night. The king was not shocked now, but worried. He said: "oh, wise man, why didn't my son come back?" The wise man answered the king: "o, generous king, your son went away before I taught him how to come back. I taught him how to make the horse go up, but not how to make the horse go down. Now he cannot come back.

The king was furious! He ordered the guards to throw the wise man in jail: "guards! Throw this man in jail, this man whom I thought was the best and wisest of the three. Throw him there because he is neither the best nor the wisest, but the worst and the dumbest! The wise man's cell was the dirtiest of the three cells.

THROW   GUARD

CELL   THE DIRTIEST CELL

Brad interrupts Fatima: "Fatima, did the Prince come back?" Fatima answered: "hear me now" and continued to tell the story: "as the Prince went higher and higher, he saw the stars become shinier and shinier, until he saw the shiniest stars. There, he could not breathe, however much he wanted to. He thought: "I can't breathe!". He looked at the mechanism and saw that it could go up, but also down. He pushed the mechanism down.

SHINY   SHINIER   SHINIEST

THE PRINCE BREATHES

STAR

Then, the horse went down. The Prince came back to the king's palace!

Jamal interrupted Fatima: "did the Persian stay in jail?" Fatima answered: "yes, he did. The Prince came back. The king, however, was still furious.

Sophia asked Fatima: "Fatima, did the other wise men marry the king's daughters?" Fatima answered: "yes, they did! Only the Persian did not marry the king's youngest daughter."

Brad asked: "Fatima, did the horse stay with the Prince?" Fatima answered: "yes, it did! The Prince and the horse travelled much together, to kingdoms further and further from Sabur's own kingdom, until the king died, and the prince came back, because he became the king."

And so, Fatima finished the story. We finish our book here too, but it is not the end. This is the first *English Patchwork* book. You can begin to read the second now!

Grammar
Comparative and superlative adjectives

The first tree is **tall;**
The second tree is **taller than** the first and **less tall than** the third;
The third tree is the **tallest** of all three.

The first cell is **dirty;**
The second cell is **dirtier than** the first and **less dirty than** the third;
The third cell is the **dirtiest** of all three.

The first tunic is **colorful;**
The second tunic is **more colorful than** the first and **less colorful than** the third;
The third tunic is the **most colorful** of all three.

Comparative adjectives compare **two things only;**
Superlative adjectives compare **three things or more;**
We add '**-er**', '**-ier**', and '**more...than**' to the adjective and form the
comparative form;

We add '**-est**', '**-iest**', and '**most**' to the adjective and form the **superlative form;**
We add '**-er**' and '**-est**' to adjectives with **only one syllable;**
We add '**-ier**' and '**-iest**' to adjectives with **two syllables whose end is -y;**
We add '**more**' and '**most**' to adjectives with **two or more syllables.**

Exercises
1. Fatima __ (↔ stops) the story: "while the king and the wise men __ about __ (< marry), the king's daughter's __ (< heard) __, because they were __ a __. The __ (= superlative < young) daughter became __ (= very angry), because she __ (< do + not) want to __ (= become a wife) the wise Persian. She __ (< run) to the __ (= place where we sleep) and __ (< tear) her __, while she screamed: __! I am __ (= very) angry!

When the __ (= son of the king) __ (< see) the __ (= daughter of the king) __ (< tear) her tunic, he __ (<come) to her and asked: 'O, __ (= daughter of my father and/or mother), why __ you __ (< tear) your tunic? You, who __ (< wear) the __ __ (< colorful) __, whose hair is the __ (= like the stars) in the kingdom, __ I see so angry?

---

stay = not move
still = until now

far, further, furthest

the reader *reads*

TALL   TALLER   TALLEST

syllable
    tall has one syllable:
    taller, talle**s**
    dir-**ty** has two syllables:
    dir**tier**, dir**tiest**
    co-lor-ful has three syllables:
    more colorful then, **most** colorful

Chapter 15 The Ebony Horse

Words

-er'
-est'
-ier'
-iest'
-st (first)
-nd (second)
- rd (third)
- th (fourth, fifth...)
away
back
bedroom
behind
good, better, best
breathe
can't
cell
clothes
colorful
continue, d
curtain
down
dumb
est
everything
from
furious
far, further, furthest
guard
high
horse
jail
little, less, least
look, ed
marriage
marry
mechanism
many, more, most
much, more, most
oh!
prince
princess
pull, ed
purple
push, ed
run, ran
read, read
ride
see, saw
shiny
shocked
sky

The princess answered: 'I am the __ (< young) daughter, however, my father wants to give me to the __ wise man!' The prince said: '__ not __ sad!', and __ (< go) to the king. The princess, however, was __ sad.

The prince said to the king: 'oh, father, why do you __ to give your __ (< young) daughter to the oldest man who __ (< come) to the __ (= king's house)?' The king answered: 'because he __ (<give) me the __ (< good) gift! __ (= see)! He gave me this __ (= black) __. It can __ in one __ the same as __ horses travel in a __.'

The prince was curious, so he __ (< say): 'oh, Persian, teach me __ to __ this horse'. The Persian __ (< teach) the prince how to go __, but not how to go __. The prince could __ the __ up, but not __ the mechanism down, so, as he went __ and __, he could not __, however __ he wanted.

As the __ (= 1:00, 2:00...) __ (< go) __, the king became __ and more __. When the __ (= 13th) hour went by, he asked: 'o, wise man, why did my son not come __?' The Persian answered: 'I taught __ (= the Prince) to go up, but not down. The prince is in the __ (=where the stars are) now. He went __ and __ (= cannot) come __ (= come to the palace again).'

The king was furious! He ordered the __ to __ the wise man in __: 'guards! throw this man in the __ __, because he is not the best nor the __ (< wise), but the __ and the __! May he __ (not move) there for a long time!'

Much, __, __. High, __, __. Worried, __ __, __ __, Dumb, __, __. Good, __, __. Bad, __, __. Shocked, __ __, __ __. Shiny, __, __. Dirty, __, __. Far, __, __. Colorful, __ __, __ __.

Pull, pulled. Push, __. Go, __. Become, __. Come, __. Speak, __. Think, __. Teach, __. Continue, __. See, __. Look, __.

The adjective co-lor-ful has three __. Its __ form is *more colorful*. Its __ form is *most colorful*. The adjective shi-ny has two __ and its end is -y. Its comparative form is __ and its superlative form is __.

2.
Who wore the most colorful clothes?
Who wore the least colorful clothes?
Why did the princess tear her tunic?
What did the prince do when he saw the princess scream and tear her tunic?
Why did the king give the youngest daughter in marriage to the oldest man?
What did the prince ask the wise man for?
What did the wise man teach the prince? What did he not teach?
How did the prince ride the horse?
Where did the prince go?
How are the stars in the highest sky like?
Did the prince come back? How?
What did the king do after the thirteenth hour went by?
Did the prince and the horse travel more?
Where did they go together?

ABOUT THE AUTHORS

Pedro Tozzi

Pedro studied classics and education at Columbia university. He is particularly fond of the way storytelling (a big social institution even today, but especially in classical societies) serves an educational purpose, making learning fun and keeping up with the memory of a society. By writing *The English Patchwork*, he aims to bring a little bit of this tradition to the contemporary world, providing students with a narrative that exposes them to relevant, inclusive content all the while teaching English literacy. Currently, he works as coordinator of the world languages department at his former high school, and as a Latin teacher, developing textbooks like this one and teaching Latin to students in his hometown, Brazil. Keeping up with the Bilingual Revolution, he learned to speak Latin and Ancient Greek, even though they are ancient languages, to better teach his students. Besides work, his hobbies include music, poetry, dancing, and video games.

Giovanna Lima

Giovanna is an illustrator from Brazil. She learned to draw by herself, practing and searching for tips and free beginners' tutorials on the internet. She began drawing realistic portraits with pencil and paper, but has been focusing on digital art since 2020. Art has been in her life since the beginning of her teenage years, at first as a hobby, helping her get through the difficulties she had to face. By illustrating "The English Patchwork" she hopes to get the attention of those who want to learn English in a fun way, with cool character design and colors that will bring to life the stories that are told throughout the book.

Besides illustrating books, she loves to draw fan art of her favorite movies and TV shows and share them with the world through social media. She loves listening to music and learning anything related to arts and crafts.

TBR Books is the publishing arm of the Center for the Advancement of Languages, Education and Communities. A non-profit organization based in New York and Paris. We publish researchers and practitioners who seek to engage diverse communities on topics related to education, languages, cultural history, and social initiatives. Our mission is to empower multilingual families and linguistic communities through education, knowledge, and advocacy. For more information, visit us at calec.org

TBR BOOKS

a program of CALEC